The UNAUTHORIZED Autobiography of W.B.

The War Years
(1933-1945)

By Walter Bodlander

The Unauthorized Autobiography of W.B.
by Walter Bodlander

Copyright 2012, Walter Boldlander

ISBN: 978-0-9654388-6-5

AZERBAIJAN
INTERNATIONAL

AZER.com

Twentieth Century Series - Vol. 1
Editor: Betty Blair

Los Angeles and Baku
ai@AZER.com

MEGA PRINT, ISTANBUL
WWW.MEGA.COM.TR

11-30-20

To Ruth,

In friendship to
you and in memory
to Art who, I wish,
might have read this —

Love

The city of Breslau had just celebrated its birthday of 1000 years when I was born there in 1920, and that's where I lived for my first 14 years. My father directed our family business—a small factory making paints, lacquers, brushes and other products needed for house painting. My great-grandfather had founded the firm in the 1830s. My mother, a typical middle-class housewife, directed our household bossing over the maid, the cook, and the governess—all young Polish women. On occasion, she would help at the office.

Breslau was less than 50 miles from the Polish border and though there was much interaction with Polish nationals, the city was proudly German. There were no Polish newspapers, no Polish billboards, no signs of Polish culture. I never heard a word of Polish spoken while I lived there. Ironically, today it is just the opposite. After WWII, the area was ceded to Poland, and the Polish government allowed no German to be spoken or printed in their newly acquired territories. All German nationals had to leave unless they agreed to these rules and their children attended Polish schools. Nearly all of them chose to leave. Breslau, now Wroclav, is today proudly Polish.

My immediate family—mother, father and uncle (my mother's brother)—considered themselves German and Prussian. Though ethnically Jewish, they were totally assimilated in the Prussian culture in which they lived. My mother's maiden name—and, of course, her brother's—was "Cohn," hyphenated as "Dembinski-Cohn," to distinguish them from the many other Cohns in the world.

Before I was even born, my uncle officially had dropped the obviously Jewish "Cohn" and shortened "Dembinski" to "Dembin."

"I shortened it for convenience," he explained. The move was not totally unusual among the "reformed" Jewish German community of that time. And it was shrewd. It helped Uncle Ernest to become a very successful businessman and the co-owner of one of Germany's largest food import and export companies.

My father did not change his name but he did change religion. That is, profoundly distrusting all organized religions, he left the Jewish community—as his father had—and officially became an atheist. Upon later reflection, I think he more likely was an agnostic.

At home God and religion were rarely mentioned. When one of my nannies announced on a Sunday morning that she was going to church, I was curious and wanted to go along. "That's fine," she said, "but ask your parents if it's ok." No one objected and so off we went to Mass. I was no older than four and remember well how I loved the huge dark church with its many paintings and sculptures. The service, probably in Latin, was completely lost on me but I was very much intrigued by a small red light hanging over the center of the altar.

"What's that?" I asked my nanny.

"That," she whispered, "is the Heart of God."

Now that was impressive and worth keeping silent for the duration of the entire hour-long religious service. From then on, we went to Mass many times until one day the nanny quit and another girl took her place.

She, too, wanted to go to church on Sunday and she, too, took me along. As we went out into the street, I ran ahead and turned left into the next street.

"No," my nanny said, "my church is to the right!"

I was deeply disappointed that we did not go to the church where the heart of God was but, of course, I went along to what obviously was the much less important church. As we entered the cathedral to my amazement, I saw a red light hanging over the altar… Now I knew that God could not have two hearts so, obviously, I had been swindled and that is when I joined my father in the firm belief that religion was a fraud. Since at that time in Germany, one had to declare one's religion when registering for school, I, too, officially became an atheist.

As a schoolboy, I liked this because when I entered Gymnasium (the school which followed the initial four years of elementary school), "religious instruction" was offered for one hour a week and I was excused. Thus, when all other students were indoctrinated with stories of Christ, Luther, or Moses, respectively, I had a free hour. In return, my father spent Sunday mornings with me reading and discussing the Old Testament and later the major German classics. I would sit on the armrest of his huge leather chair while we read Schiller's epic poems, Goethe's *Faust* and all Lessing's plays. This tradition started when I was five years old and ended only when I had to leave for Switzerland 10 years later.

We lived mid-town in a huge eight-room apartment on the second floor. While most affluent families began to move to the more modern suburbs, my father stubbornly insisted on staying where we were because it was within walking distance to the factory. For me it was a serious disadvantage. No children lived nearby. Although I had made a number of friends at school, all of them lived in the outskirts of town and getting together was difficult.

In the first years of my childhood, I felt painfully lonely and isolated. Happily, this changed when on my 11th birthday I was allowed to join the Boy Scouts. Then every weekend I was in the company of peers and I loved every moment of it. I was by far the youngest in my group but I was completely accepted by my teen-age comrades. My scout name was "Meterman"—although I was at least 25 cm taller than the mere three feet my nickname implied.

Weekend outings began Saturday afternoon with a train ride to some village and from there a hike into fields and forest. Each of us carried a knapsack with tent equipment, a two-day supply of food, extra clothing and toiletries. For me, the pack seemed heavy and the hike—six to 10 miles—was often exhausting. But I was honor-bound not to complain and to keep up with my friends. When we would arrive in the wilderness at a place deemed acceptable by our leader, we would pitch our tents, build a bonfire, sing folk songs about the Thirty-Year War and play endurance games.

There were many tests to pass. At night one might be left alone in the forest with a compass and instructions to find one's way back to camp without the use of a flashlight. Or one had to jump over a huge campfire—at the risk of getting burned. And there were daytime tasks, many seemed—or actually were—dangerous, but they had to be mastered.

Sometimes there were special ceremonies together with other scout troops. We would march to a clearing in the forest to the meeting place. To fife and drum, we would line up forming a large square. Then while we were standing at attention, the music would stop. All would be very quiet. After a while, a trumpet would sound and one of the leaders would step into the square and begin the ceremony. There were loyalty oaths, short speeches, joint songs, friendship and camaraderie.

It was all very romantic, very fraternal, very militaristic. The overall goal of scouting was to stretch one's endurance to the ultimate, conquer physical fear, bond with one's comrades and evoke national pride. For me, it absolutely succeeded. The flames of patriotism consumed me. As a boy between 11 and 13, I was a good German. A proud German.

I did not know that I was Jewish until one day in 1933. This was the year the Nazis came to power. And this was the year my father talked to me about the political situation.

"You may know," he said, "that the new regime considers people to be Jews not only if they are religious, but also by race. Anyone who has a Jewish father, mother, grandfather or grandmother is considered Jewish. Period. That means that we are Jewish in their eyes and, therefore, disliked and disempowered.

That this is total nonsense is not important. The Nazis are now in power and they set the rules. So we will conduct ourselves as Jews, consider ourselves Jews, even if we don't follow Jewish religious doctrines. We will not hide our heritage. We will be proud of it and never deny it."

Then he asked me if I had any questions. "Are all our relatives also Jews?" I asked.

"Wow, amazing!"

And I found out that most of our friends were Jews as well. To the merriment of my mother, I noted: "I didn't know there were so many Jews in the world."

So, overnight, I became a proud German Jew.

It was then that I became aware of the increasing and blatant anti-Semitic propaganda. Signs appeared in restaurants: "Jews will not be served here." Want ads in newspapers included "Jews need not apply." By 1934 the obscene propaganda sheet *Der Stürmer* published by Julius Streicher was publicly displayed in many parks and squares.

This was an outrageously vicious scandal sheet. The front page always featured a cartoon of an ugly, bearded, hook-nosed Jew salivating while raping a blond Arian defenseless girl. And the so-called news stories told of ritual murders and other atrocities that Jews had recently committed. All disgusting fabrications. Fortunately, Streicher was captured after the war, condemned at Nuremberg and hanged.

To my 13-year-old mind, all this anti-Semitism was simply a sign of ignorance. If only people knew how truly German we Jews were, how heroically we would fight for the Fatherland... etc... etc. This adolescent attitude lasted for a couple of years and was reinforced by the fact that I personally was never harassed. The name "Bodlander" did not sound Jewish, and my light brown hair and blue eyes did not fit the stereotype.

Soon, however, things began to change. At school, new history books about World War I were added to the curriculum. Now we learned of the treachery of the Social Democratic and

Communist parties—both, of course, under the leadership of Jews, which resulted in the abominable Weimar Republic and the loss of the war. Had it not been for their villainous stab in the back of the nation in the last minute ("*Dolchstoss*"), we would surely have won the war.

"Stab-in-the-Back" was a reference to the fact that the new German government had agreed to the November 11th Armistice (1918) and accepted the Versailles Peace Treaty (1919). That the German Army High Command had urged the Kaiser to accept the Armistice because the Army was totally exhausted and essential war supplies were no longer available was, of course, not mentioned.

The Jews were the bane of the German nation. This revised history was now endlessly discussed and fervently taught. The Hitler Youth—previously an organization competing with the Boy Scouts—became the only authorized youth movement. The Scouts were disbanded—as were all political parties, except the NSDAP (Nazis). Private clubs, lodges and groups like the Elks, were gradually integrated into the Nazi hierarchy. Jews, formerly members in good standing, were now excluded.

With the Boy Scouts disbanded, I joined a newly formed youth group of secular Jews. We were tolerated by the government because only Jews could belong. We were not allowed to wear any uniform so we all wore white shirts and black short trousers. Generally, this organization continued where the Scouts had left off. My nickname changed from "Meterman" to "Em". Otherwise, all was about the same as before. We called ourselves the "Black Pennant", held weekly club meetings and weekend outings.

It was on one of these night marches that a newfound friend talked to me about Communism. He explained Marx's ideas to me that workers should have the right to own the tools of production and receive the full benefit of their labor. Under the present system, he pointed out, the worker was exploited and received only a fraction of the wealth he produced. Look at the terrible failure of the capitalist system. Indeed, the world was in the midst of the Great Depression. I knew there was unemployment and discontent all around me—both at home and abroad. I had read the news stories of farmers in America pouring buckets of milk into the gutter in the very streets where starving people were standing in long lines in hope of getting some free food.

As we marched in the darkness, my friend spoke of the incredible poverty in Brazil and Argentina where boatloads of bananas were thrown into the ocean so that the price of the fruit would go up. He spoke of the aim of the Communist Party to give equal rights to women, the rights for workers to organize into unions in order to get better wages, the need for the central distribution of goods, so that everyone could have equal access to them. The lecture lasted all night and I became totally convinced. It all sounded fair and right.

What could be more beautiful than the Communist motto: "From each according to his ability, to each according to his needs." Yes, I wanted to work for a world where everyone would be able to work to the best of his ability, just as we all had worked together in our Scout group—a world of equals, with equal rights and equal responsibilities. Greed and laziness would be overcome to the benefit of all.

Though I see the world differently today than when I was 14, I never lost my left-wing orientation. The need to rectify as much as possible of the man-made injustices of society has never left me.

My ardent German nationalism, on the other hand, luckily, did not last very long. Soon, I understood the dangers and absurdity of Nazi politics. The main opponents of this hateful ideology were the Communists and Socialists. I considered myself one of them.

By 1935, the situation was changing again. The anti-Semitic Nuremberg Laws were passed. New quotas were set, limiting the number of Jews allowed to enter various professions including law, entertainment, journalism, and finance. The first concentration camp at Dachau was opened and now arrests of "political enemies" became more frequent. Rumors circulated that treatment at Dachau was extremely harsh, occasionally fatal. Prisoners served sentences of undetermined lengths, some were released after a few months, but some were held for years. Some never got out.

In schools and universities all classes now had to begin and end with the Nazi salute: "*Heil Hitler*", And in the streets, one was expected to enter and leave shops greeting others with "*Heil Hitler*", instead of "Good Morning" or "Good Bye".

The unemployed began to find jobs throughout Germany because they were building the "autobahn".

My family was now seriously considering leaving Germany. Maps of Poland, France and Czechoslovakia appeared at the dinner table: What country would be safest and best? Where and how could we make a living? Did one have to learn a new language? Would one be accepted? Endless questions and no satisfactory answers.

Above all these deliberations there always loomed the most essential question: Is emigration the right decision? Life in Germany for Jews was bad but was it really THAT bad? How much longer could this bankrupt regime last? When would the people throw the Nazis out? And if we were to leave, we would have to sell our business. Who would buy a Jewish business? And at what depressed price?

To stay or to emigrate was the most difficult decision to make and was further complicated by the devilish tactics Hitler used in both domestic and international affairs. He did not proclaim: "We will kill the 600,000 German Jews this year," nor did he order the conquest of all of Europe immediately for the benefit of his Arian race. Instead, he moved slowly, step by step, and after completing each step successfully, he would announce to the world that now his demands had been met. He was satisfied, now there could be peace.

The international steps are history: the re-building of the Army, the creation of the Air Force, (both breaches of the Versailles Treaty), the militarization of the West Bank of the Rhine, the annexation of the Saar (after a fraudulent plebiscite), the construction of submarines, the annexation of Austria and on and on. Every one of these breaches of promises or treaties was followed by the solemn declaration that this was his last demand. In the domestic arena, regarding the Jews, he followed the same tactic. Each new restrictive decree was "the last" and often it was sugarcoated with some "fair" provision. For instance, the Nuremberg Laws forbade Jews to fly the German flag, but they were specifically allowed to fly a Jewish flag. Jewish lawyers had to be dismissed if an office had over-filled the new quotas, but, on the other hand, the dismissed lawyers could work as paralegals.

Now, even if one had decided to leave everything behind, two more incredibly important problems were added. One was strictly financial. Though the Nazis "encouraged" Jews to leave, they imposed a very heavy "Fugitive Tax" on all assets that Jews wanted to take out of Germany. Furthermore, the currency (German Mark) had to be exchanged into the foreign currency at an artificially low rate, thus imposing an additional tax. The result was that an owner of an estate worth 10,000 Marks ended up with less than 3,000 that could be taken to the new country.

Another enormous obstacle was getting a visa or entry permit to anywhere. The world was in a depression. No one wanted immigrants for whom there would be no work. Many countries demanded that stiff financial requirements be met before an entry visa would be granted and even then, most had long waiting lists.

The more these questions came up, the more the inclination to wait. Did you really want to abandon all your friends, your acquaintances and clubs, your home, the library, the theater and restaurants? Did you want to exchange a bourgeois life style for a gypsy-like existence? Was it wise to give up a comfortable and, at least, for now, tolerable life style for a very uncertain future?

Early in 1934 Jews were ordered to surrender their passports temporarily so that they could be stamped with a large red "I" for Isidor and "S" for Sarah—both Jewish names. To avoid this without directly disobeying orders, my uncle and his best friend Mr. Markus, a lawyer, went abroad for a few days to nearby Czechoslovakia. There they discussed whether they should stay in

Germany or leave forever. They could not make up their minds and finally decided to take the advice from a mutual friend, a very prominent Breslau judge, a Christian. They phoned him and asked him to meet them in Czechoslovakia.

He came and when he heard the question they asked him, he replied: "You must be out of your mind. How can you think of leaving Germany. You are both important people in the community. This Nazi nonsense will not last more than a few months."

That settled the problem and they returned home. My parents found a compromise. They decided to stay but to send me to school in Switzerland. This was very good news for me. I was not happy at home. I felt isolated and lonely. At school I was enrolled in the Humanist section of the Gymnasium: lots of Latin and Greek, German History, with a minimum of Math, Sciences and the Arts.

I had been enrolled in elementary school early and, thus, at the Gymnasium (High School), I was always the youngest and smallest. Not good in Germany. I was the brunt of bad jokes and got bullied a lot. Some of my teachers were rather nasty and dismissive. Besides, my grades were, at best, mediocre. I remember showing my mother (upon demand) the latest exam papers, often, alas, marked with a "D" or "Fail". She would look at the marks, and then with a disgusted glance, raise her eyes to heaven and silently implore the gods as to why they had burdened her with such a hopeless son. Today, I assume that this must have been her idea of energizing me towards studying more, but at the time I did not take it well at all.

2

The decision was made to enroll me in a school in Neuchatel, a student town in the French-speaking part of Switzerland. For three months prior to leaving I took private French lessons every Saturday. When the day came to leave Breslau, my parents were at the train station—my father restrained, my mother in tears, and I, elated and excited to begin this great adventure. Seeing my mother's tears, I admonished her: "Don't cry, you're spoiling the pleasure of my departing." Evidently, this cut deeply. Years later, she often reminded me of this "bon-mot".

Mr. and Mrs. Weber ran a small *"pension"* for foreign students. Their house—built on top of a vineyard—overlooked the town and Lake Neuchatel. The house was called "Clos Fleuri" (Flowering Corner). It was a charming, friendly place. We were five students at the Weber pension: three English boys, myself, and François—another German Jew. Being an only child, it was my first experience to live with people my age. I loved it.

The Webers were good foster parents. He was a high school teacher; she, a housewife, taking care of her five wards, a husband, and a cat. They were in there 30s and seemed to honestly like us kids. For the first time, I experienced a feeling of family life. Usually, after the evening meal, we would all sit around the table and play Monopoly or some card games or just talk. Of course, it was all in French. At first we didn't understand each other but with humor and gestures we managed to get along and soon we began to improve our language skills. It's interesting how quickly a foreign language can be learned if one is young and completely immersed in the new language.

I was enrolled in the "Ecole Superieure de Commerce"—a four-year-school, ending with a "Diplome", the equivalent of a two-year-college degree. Foreign students were placed in a special program, which consisted of a very intensive and exclusive study of French—six hours a day. From the beginning, it was expected that we would be fluent enough in French to join regular classes within six months. Happily, I learned the language quickly and soon participated in the regular program.

As was customary in those years, Ecole de Commerce was only for boys. But Neuchatel was a student town. In addition to my school, Neuchatel had a university and several girls' schools. Consequently, the town catered to young people. It had many cafés and dance halls, several movie houses and a theater. Evenings, especially on weekends, were lively. After homework was done, we were allowed to go out. The Webers imposed a curfew of 10 p.m.

Twice a year, on Christmas and summer vacations, I went home to Breslau. The train ride took 14 hours and was always an exciting adventure. At Basel, the Swiss border, there was usually a delay of two hours. All major train stations had restaurants—often, the best ones in town. The Basel restaurant was one of the finest and I always looked forward to eating there. Their specialty was "Hors d'Oevres". The waiter would roll several carts to the table, each cart filled with rows of wonderful dishes from which one could take a sample. Traveling alone, at 15, I felt very grown up.

On short holidays, when the English students went home, the Webers took Francois and me on day trips to the Swiss Alps or the Jura Mountains.

Both 1935 and 1936 passed both happily and uneventfully. I had made friends with Francois and with Cyril, a student at my school. His parents were Russian emigrants now living in German-speaking Switzerland, and he, like me, had been sent to Neuchatel to learn French. Many evenings the three of us went to movies and then to one of the cafes for a beer and talk. We gawked at girls and talked politics.

The Café du Theatre—our main meeting place—had Swiss, German and French newspapers available to customers. We could go there, have a beer or a cup of coffee, and read or just sit as long as we wanted. Except for Saturday nights, there never was any pressure to give up one's table. The international situation, particularly developments in Germany, were front-page stories, which we discussed endlessly and with passion.

In September 1936, everything changed. I received a telegram to come home immediately—my father was very ill. On the train home, someone had left a paper and there I saw the obituary for my father. He had died of a heart attack the previous day. I got home in time for services and—according to his wishes—the cremation. It was a terrible blow.

I knew my father had a heart condition, and that his doctor had asked him not to smoke, but dad had not taken that advice seriously. I remember how he often would walk with an unlit cigarette between his lips, and when admonished by my mother, he would smile: "Look, I'm not smoking," but then, a little later, the cigarette mysteriously got lit and smoked. And I knew, of course, of the worries and anxieties he bore, created by the political situation. That pressure clearly was too much and now it was over. The many questions I had wanted to ask him were never asked or answered. He was a very good man—a wise man—and much admired by friends and acquaintances, much missed by mother and me.

I went back to school a few days later. My mother was now in charge of the family business and was trying to sell it.

3

In the summer of 1937, I came down with a rather obscure ailment called Iritis, an inflammation of the iris. If not promptly treated, I was told it could lead to blindness. It had affected one eye. The school sent me to an outstanding ophthalmologist who had me hospitalized for tests because he was certain that some blood infection had caused the inflammation. A few days later my other eye became infected as well. All tests were inconclusive. Ears, nose, teeth, and all organs were examined, nothing seemed wrong. A staff of doctors worked on me, but they could not locate the cause of the infection nor of the slight continuous fever.

Hospitalized now for over a week with both eyes bandaged and confronted with the possibility of going blind, my ophthalmologist asked permission to try an experimental treatment. I would receive an injection of raw milk, which would induce a very high fever, which might kill the infection and save my eyes. The risk was that the fever could not be controlled, it might affect my brain and that the infection might not be killed. What if we did nothing? I would certainly lose my sight shortly. There was no time to waste, I was told. No time to contact my mother. So I gave my consent.

The injection was extremely painful and the fever lasted for several days. I was told later that I had been unconscious for about a week. When I came to, with both eyes bandaged, I slept most of the time. One day the bandages from one eye were removed and, vaguely, I could see the smiling face of my doctor. Soon the other eye improved as well and as the iris healed, I was released from the hospital. Six weeks had passed.

With immense gratitude to my doctor, I resumed my studies. But the blood infection was still there, manifested by a continuous low fever. That Christmas my mother insisted I come home. In Breslau, our family physician immediately hospitalized me for further tests. The first question he asked me was: "Did they check your tonsils in Neuchatel?"

"Of course," I said, "that was their first suspicion and I had told them that my tonsils had been removed years ago."

"Not removed," said my doctor. "Capped."

He checked them and found that the remaining tonsils were badly infected. Within a day, I had my second tonsillectomy. By mid-January of 1938, I was ready to go back to Neuchatel, completely healed. That was my last time in Breslau. Life here had changed dramatically, and for Jews, much for the worse. Signs: "Boycott the Jews" or "Jews and Dogs Not Allowed" appeared in many places. More and more professions were closed to Jews, physical attacks on Jews and suspected opponents to the Nazis were frequent, and one heard constantly that people had been taken into "Schutzhaft" (protective custody), i.e., a concentration camp.

The "German Salute"—the outstretched arm followed by a loud declaration "Heil Hitler" was now commonplace everywhere. As a matter of fact, one entered and left shops with "Heil Hitler". Jews were exempt from this but, of course, failing to salute automatically identified them either "enemies of the state" or as Jews. Many participated in this madness simply to remain anonymous.

There was virtually no more unemployment. Young and old were working in re-armament, now an open secret. The State and the Party, of course, needed funding, so in addition to the regular taxes, there was a constant demand for money. Party members stood with tin boxes on nearly every street corner asking passers-by to contribute. One was expected to give all one's change and, in return, was given a small lapel pin indicating that they need not give again the same week. During fall and winter, the donations supposedly were for *"Winterhilfswerk"*—to help those few still unemployed during intemperate winter days. In spring and summer, one was expected to "give" for the financing of the future Volkswagen. Hitler had promised that soon every German would be able to afford his own Nazi-built car.

Public air raid shelters had been constructed and signs directing one to the nearest location were prominently displayed. Every city block had a designated warden in charge of evacuation and fire prevention. Each home had to be prepared to be blacked out so that no light could be seen outside. All windows had to be criss-crossed with tape so that the glass would not shatter. In fact, all shop windows were taped like this.

Germany was ready for war.

The trip back to Neuchatel was not without peril. Rumors had it that at the border, teen-age boys were being detained until it was determined that they were not draft-dodgers. My passport had been stamped with a large red "I" for "Isidor", the official name given to all Jewish males. Though Jews were not accepted into the armed services, they had to register with the draft board. Actually, nothing happened. The border crossing was uneventful.

At the Webers, mail was awaiting me from the German Consulate in Zurich. It was a form to fill out in order to receive an exemption from the draft while studying in Switzerland. Of course, I had no intention of serving in the German army but I did fill out the form dutifully and sent it back together with two passport photos. A second letter came from the Consulate stating that they could not process my application because I had furnished only two photos, when three had been requested. Well, I did not have another photo, so I did not bother and they never got their third photo. A few weeks later, they notified me that I had lost my German citizenship due to attempted desertion. So now I was "Stateless"—a condition not enviable in 1938 Europe. My passport expired in November 1938 and, of course, I would not be issued a new one.

Sometime earlier, in May 1938, the Nazis decreed that no more money could be sent out of Germany not even to pay for education abroad. My tuition had been pre-paid until graduation, but the room and board fees to the Webers were sent monthly and now that had to stop. The Monsieur told me that I could stay until June but then I would have to leave.

Every month, my parents had sent me some pocket money and always counseled me to try to save as much as possible. I found saving a tedious business but had managed to put away a few francs. Now, one year prior to graduation I had saved enough to last until graduation, provided I did not spend more that 160 francs a month.

I found a room for rent—60 franks a month, including breakfast. It was a good deal and close to school. Mme. Faitu, the landlady, agreed to my request to serve the "breakfast" at night— an egg, toast and coffee. Thus, I had a guaranteed hot dinner brought to my room punctually at 7 pm on a neat little wooden tray.

That summer it was not advisable to go back to Breslau. Rumors circulated that Jews of military age who entered Germany were being retained—their fate unknown. This gave me a perfect excuse to stay in Switzerland and to take a bicycle trip with a friend to Lugano. Since this meant crossing the Alps, we stored our bikes almost immediately and began to hitchhike. This was very much less strenuous and a lot more exciting. It was also contrary to parental admonition. We both got separate rides almost immediately and wound up happily at the lake of this beautiful city.

Descending the Alps, I experienced for the first time, the warm climate of southern Europe with its palm trees and—what was for me—exotic flora. The beauty was intoxicating. As I arrived in Lugano, I walked to one of the many parks and sat there for several hours engulfed in the romanticism of the tropical south. This first encounter with a Mediterranean environment deeply impressed me. Love at first sight. So different from the cold Breslau and even the temperate Neuchatel.

By the end of that summer, central Europe was in turmoil. In spring, Germany had moved into Austria ("*Anschluss*") as unopposed by western democracies as it had been when it had moved into the Saar and the Rhineland earlier. A glance at the map made it clear that Czechoslovakia, now practically surrounded by Germany, would be the next target. France and the Soviet Union announced that any threat to that country would lead to war.

By mid-August, the Nazi propaganda machine wrote on a daily basis of terrible crimes committed by Czech citizens against German nationals living in the Czech-owned Sudetenland. In ever more shrill and hysterical speeches, Hitler demanded that "these crimes must stop or my army will have to take matters into its own hands, and impose order and secure safety for German nationals."

Not coincidentally, all the Czech defense lines and most of their heavy industry were located in the very area Hitler was now threatening. War—feared by everyone, including the neutral Swiss—seemed inevitable. Hitler demanded an immediate solution to what he deemed was an untenable situation. The French Premier Daladier, and his British counterpart Chamberlain, wrung their hands. Meetings were called at Berchtesgaden. Chamberlain met Hitler at Bad Godesberg but the *Fuehrer* insisted on an immediate German army presence in the Sudetenland to discipline the "Czech hoodlums".

Newspapers reported daily about on-going war preparations. Soviet, French, Italian, and British armies were mobilizing—readying themselves for war. It seemed that finally the Allies were standing their ground. Hitler would be stopped or war was inevitable.

Then on the evening of September 30, as Mrs. Faitu brought me my daily "breakfast", we heard over the radio that an agreement had just been reached among the major powers and that war had been averted. Indeed, the previous day, England, France and Italy had met with Hitler at Munich, and after negotiating for less than a day, they had accepted Germany's demands. Hitler was allowed to occupy the Sudetenland. The crisis was over.

This was the infamous Munich Conference. Chamberlain flew home to London and announced jubilantly: "Peace in our time"' and Mr. Daladier complained in Paris that he had been outvoted. Hitler told the world that now all his demands had been met, he had no further quarrels. Mme. Faitu was relieved that there would be no war. I was outraged at the betrayal of Czechoslovakia and the cowardice of the West.

It is important to note—but rarely mentioned in articles of that time—that neither the Soviet Union—then a major ally of France—nor Czechoslovakia had been invited to Munich. Nor were they ever asked to agree to that atrocious surrender. That the very country whose fate was to be decided was not even allowed to be present at the deliberations is unforgivable.

But the fact that the Soviet Union was not allowed to participate speaks volumes of the intent of France and England to agree—or rather, not to agree—to the Soviets' constant plea for collective resistance to Hitler's aggressions. The stage was now set for Hitler to march into Prague any time convenient and, indeed, German tanks did roll through the Czech capital, unopposed, the following March (1939),

The next victim was already in the news: Poland. According to the screaming German press communiqués, Poland was committing atrocities against German nationals, and Danzig, an independent city inside Poland, demanded to be "returned to the Reich." It was now—in February 1939—that England and France announced that, indeed, they would accept the Soviet Union's invitation to a joint meeting. The purpose: to forge a military alliance aimed to stop any further German aggression and territorial demands. For years Litvinov, the Foreign Minister of the Soviet Union, had advocated such an alliance in the League of Nations.

"Collective Security" was the name given to the proposed pact and it was endlessly "discussed" but never seriously considered by either Britain or France. Now finally the three nations would meet to forge a formal military treaty. The Conference was to be held in Leningrad by the end of February. England asked for additional time to prepare. Three weeks went by. Finally a date was agreed upon. The French representatives had flown into the city but the British were delayed. They had decided to go by boat. As the Conference finally got under way, it became clear that neither the French nor the English delegates had the authority to enter into any meaningful agreements. The reluctance—not to mention the insincerity of the West to deal seriously together with the Soviet Union—was rather evident. Stalin, not known for being patient, lost whatever patience he had and put an end to the Conference in late April.

On May 3, 1939, Litvinov was dismissed and replaced with Molotov. The change meant that a new Soviet foreign policy was in the making. Since the West clearly was not interested to stop Hitler, and since the aggressive German intentions against the Soviet Union had been announced for decades, there was only one hope available to Stalin to gain time and rearm as quickly as possible. He would try to engage Germany.

On August 23, 1939, Molotov and Ribbentrop signed the German-Soviet Non-Aggression Pact, a document as ludicrously insincere and sarcastically self-serving, as any in world history. Now Hitler was assured he would never have to fight simultaneously a war on two fronts and Stalin got time for more effective defense.

4

The "patinoire" (ice skating rink) at Neuchatel had been opened in 1937 and was an immediate success. Not that an ice-skating rink was anything so special—even Breslau had not one but several. The Breslau rinks were part of the mote, which had been built about 800 A.D. to serve the city as protection and as a sewerage system. As the town grew beyond the mote, bridges were needed and eventually, the mote was dissected into six or seven separate waterways connected by underground pipes to the Oder River—and mercifully no longer used as a sewer system.

In winter, as each section froze, the city opened the waterways for ice-skating. One paid a few pfennigs as entrance fee, was yelled at by underpaid attendants responsible for the glaring music piped over loudspeakers, and was subjected to their main entertainment: that of making young people miserable. Everything fun was "verboten"—playing tag, shouting, racing, boisterous laughing, even pushing girls and pulling their hair—all forbidden. Nonetheless, I went a few times a week and became a reasonably good skater.

So the Neuchatel rink was a welcome addition. And it was also quite special: it was one of Switzerland's first outdoor rinks with artificial ice. It did not operate year round, but it opened at the beginning of school in September, long before natural ice was available and it closed in May. Surrounded by a few "in" cafes and dance places, it became a major social center for the city's student population.

I suppose every student town has its quota of beautiful girls—mysterious, desirable, delectable, and untouchable. Among that very select group, there is always one who outshines all others. She's the girl on everyone's mind—the one with long flowing hair, with silvery voice, easy crystalline laugh, magnificent body, the one more beautiful than words can describe, the one guys barely dare to smile at for fear of a condescending shrug, the one so far out of reach that a date with the moon is easier to imagine. In Neuchatel in 1938, her name was Jeanette.

What I knew of her was very little and that was both good news and bad. She was a local girl—good news. It meant she would be here next year. But she was Harry Huber's girl—very bad news, indeed. Harry was a Swiss from Zurich and very, very rich. We were classmates and acquaintances, but Harry was a playboy, bright and carefree, and his circle of friends did not mix with mine who were considered the intelligentsia of the Ecole de Commerce.

The best way to describe Harry's status is in one sentence: He drove his own car to school. In 1937 in Neuchatel that would have been equivalent to a student in 1999 flying his own helicopter. Harry never spoke of Jeanette to me and, of course, I never asked him. And since she was not a classmate, not even a schoolmate, I never saw her except at the "patinoire". There she would skate easily, hair flowing, skirt blowing as she would end a routine in a beautiful pirouette. She would always come alone and leave alone but she was always surrounded by Harry and his friends. That is where I first saw her—the previous season—skating to the most romantic music, floating as if on ice. OK, she was on ice and she was a sight I could not forget.

It was a week or so after Munich that my friend Francois stopped by my room. "We're all going to the patinoire this afternoon, why don't you come along?"

"Who is 'we all'"?

"Well… Cyril, Erica, John and me and, of course, Harry and his friends. It's his birthday and he's buying beer for everyone. So they say."

Free beer is nothing to be laughed at when you have no money, but the fact that Harry would be there was decisive. My stringent budget allowed for one skating outing a month and my fear was that I would pick an evening when Jeanette was not there. Today, obviously, was the right day. So we took our bicycles. Harry arrived in his car—a white convertible. After skating for an hour, Jeanette almost crashed into me twice and once actually brushed my hand as we were skating in opposite directions.

Harry called out: "We're going to Yverdon for dinner. Come and join us."

Yverdon, a small picturesque village at the lake was about 45 minutes by bike. I was thinking that I needed time to study, and that dinner and beer were really beyond my budget when two miracles took place. As Harry was discussing plans, he said: "Hey, beer and sandwiches are on me. It's my birthday, after all. And we'll open the car, so we have room for six. So, Walter, why don't you come with us and leave the bike here?"

As we piled into the convertible tightly squeezed, Jeanette suddenly jumped on my lap. "I hope you don't mind," she said. "I thought you'd sit in front with Harry" is all I could think of in reply. "Oh, that's long over," she said, "he's a creep." And then she whispered: "Never did like him anyway."

We all danced a lot that night in Yverdon and probably drank much too much beer. It was an intoxicating night but it was not the alcohol that caused it. Love was in the air and we both knew something wonderful was beginning. There were a number of girls in our party but the only dancing partner I remember was Jeanette. By 11 p.m., Harry brought everyone back to the patinoire to pick up their bikes. As we said good night, Harry gave me an odd look, which I interpreted as a mixture of surprise and begrudging respect.

Beaux Arts was the address of Mme. Faitu's apartment. It was on the ground floor and my room was in the back. The window opened onto a park-like garden, framed by the block's apartment houses and, thus, forming a large square. Beautiful arched gateways opened onto the streets on all four sides. Thus, there was no need for me to go through Mme. Faitu's foyer when I wanted to leave or come home. My window—always open—became my door. But it never was a door for Jeanette.

We met almost daily but only once did she come to my window. It was quite early in our relationship. I was doing homework late in the afternoon and had trouble concentrating because I was hungry and waiting for my "breakfast". Suddenly, a tap on the window.

"Hi," said Jeanette, "my father is away today so I can go out tonight. Mum doesn't care, so I don't need to go home for dinner. What do you say?"

The window was open but she was not quite tall enough and had to stand on her toes to look in.

"Here," I said, "stand on this, and I gave her a chair." Now she was tall enough so we could kiss. It was a long, sweet, "in-love" type of kiss, somewhat awkward since now on her chair, she was taller than I—but like all our kisses, it was timeless and forever. When we finally broke away, I said: "Great, I just need to change my shirt. Climb in."

"No," she said, a little too fast, "but I'll watch."

"Well, maybe you'd like to change your blouse and wear one of my shirts and I'll watch."

"No thanks," she smiled. "Come here, you bastard."

By now she was sitting on the windowsill, sidesaddle, her legs still outside. We kissed again and so wildly that somehow a few of the buttons of her blouse became undone—and then there was a knock at the door and Mme. Faitu appeared with a tray of hot coffee, a boiled egg, and two pieces of buttered toast.

"Well, hello," she smiled at Jeanette; and to me, she offered: "Dinner is served."

She left as suddenly as she had come, but the spell was broken.

Much later Jeanette told me that she was not sure whether she was glad or angry that Mme. Faitu had shown up. "I was about to jump in, you know, and we would have been in big trouble."

She never came to the window again. The innocence of those years must be very hard for young people today to understand. At that time I did not know of any pregnant students and those years were long before the pill—but none of the girls I knew were married. It was not because of Victorian prudishness, but more like a respect for privacy, and inhibitions, fueled by fear of unwanted pregnancies.

I was never very good with money—or perhaps, better said—I was very good with it, indeed, and loved to spend it, occasionally even when I did not have it. At this time, budgeting was important and not too difficult. Of the monthly 160 francs available—60 went to Mme. Faitu, 3 daily for me to spend. Not a lot because I needed to buy occasional schoolbooks and supplies and, of course, stamps to write to my mother. A halfway reasonable lunch could be had for 1 Fr, 75. That then left a few centimes daily to accumulate for an occasional movie or a glass of beer with friends.

What about Jeanette? Easy. Love won over lunch, and my lunch money went for wine with my girl. Interestingly enough, the Webers who had been very nice and parental all these years never invited me for lunch or dinner. They never even contacted me, and I certainly did not want to appear to be begging so I never called on them.

Then I met Hans Levi. He, too, was a German Jewish student at the Ecole de Commerce. I had not known him because he was in a different section. We met accidentally at the college bookstore and discovered that we both were in the same predicament. No more money from home and little savings. I told him of my break-fast-dinner arrangement, and he told me that he survived from food packages his parents sent him almost daily.

Since he had enough food for two, we agreed to combine forces. We would meet for lunch: he would provide the spread and I, the bread. Daily bread, butter and coffee cost less than 50 centimes. Suddenly, I had plenty of money for evenings with Jeanette. Unfortunately, my association with Hans did not last very long. He graduated in February and Swiss immigration informed him that his student visa had expired. He was to leave promptly. By May they caught up with him and gave him 10 days to leave the country.

Switzerland had gained a reputation of benevolence due probably to its fierce insistence on independence and its strict neutrality in European conflicts. But the Swiss were not quite as benevolent when it came to foreigners whose visas had expired. Fully aware of the plight of German Jews, they made no exceptions. An expired visa meant deportation to the country of origin.

However, rather than sending them back to Germany, they gave German Jews a choice as to which country they wished to go, providing it bordered Switzerland. The choices were Austria (by then under the control of Nazis), Fascist Italy (a close ally with Hitler), or France. The choice was obvious.

I had heard rumors about other students in this situation. They had been sent to France, arrested at the French-Swiss border for entering France without a visa. There they spent a few days in custody and then were sent back to Switzerland, simply to be put back again on a train heading to France again. Eventually, no doubt, they ended up in a French internment camp. This was what Hans was now facing. He disappeared and I have no idea what happened to him. After the French army was defeated in 1940, these camps were closed. The inmates, mostly German and Austrian Jews were sent to Germany as forced labor and later to feed the ovens at the extermination camps.

One can hardly blame Mr. Hofer—Jeanette's dad—for his fiendish rules. A postal functionary of middle rank, he could be sure of two things: he would never be fired and he would never be rich. Rich, in the sense of "well-off". That meant that his only child, Jeanette—thank God, a very pretty girl—was to marry an honorable suitable Swiss lad—someone from a Calvinist family with a recognizable name and a position in life to guarantee her a comfortable existence. Therefore, dad had established three cardinal rules for her: (1) Do not date foreigners. (2) Do not date Catholics—Jews were not even mentioned. (3) Any boy you date for the third time must be brought home for approval.

When Mr. Hofer heard that Jeanette had broken off with Harry, he was pleased to note that, for the time being at least, she seemed to have lost interest in boys. Sure, she went out two or three times a week but these were evenings with girlfriends or outings to movies. She never mentioned a "date", never mentioned interest in anyone, and when asked, she just shrugged her shoulders and said: "I have a lot of studying to do and much on my mind."

"Heartbroken over Harry," Mr. Hofer confided to his wife. "We'd best just leave her alone."

Thus, I never met Jeanette's frightful father, never could go to her home, never could even call her on the phone. But we did meet several times a week in the evenings. Neuchatel had a number of cafés and our place was the Rotonde, a charming little spot near the lake. Always full of young people, the lively atmosphere was enhanced by a small dance band. Early in our relationship, we had gone there and when the orchestra started a waltz I confessed that I did not know how to dance it.

"I'll teach you," said Jeanette, bravely exposing her feet to my clumsy attempts to master the dance. The bandleader must have spotted us because he began to laugh and repeated the melody for quite some time until he felt I had at least learned the basic steps. The tune was called "The Umbrella Man" and, of course, it became "our song".

We made friends with Maurice, the bandleader, and eventually a very special private code evolved. When I came to the restaurant, I would look at Maurice and if he changed the music to the "Umbrella Man", I would know Jeanette was already there. But if I arrived first, the music would continue, I'd find a table. Nursing my beer, I would wait for the "Umbrella Man" to herald Jeanette's arrival.

These were the years of the Spanish Civil War and just before I had met Jeanette, I had gotten deeply involved in that conflict. I followed the battlefield news daily. For me, there had never been a war so clear-cut. It was obvious who were the good guys and who, the bad. Franco, a pro-Fascist general had led a group of disgruntled troops from Spanish Morocco to overthrow the democratic government in Madrid. They landed in Spain and were immediately assisted—both in weapons and soldiers—by Mussolini and Hitler, who welcomed a potential new Fascist state in Europe.

Such intervention was against the rules of the League of Nations and could have been stopped immediately by economic sanctions or military action against Germany and Italy. Instead of assisting the legitimately elected democratic government of Spain, both England and France nobly decided to remain "neutral" thus facilitating the death of the Spanish Republic. Only the Soviet Union stood squarely on the side of the "Loyalists" and sent weapons and ammunitions.

Outraged by the inaction of Western democracies and the unfairness of the situation, well-intentioned people the world over came to volunteer for the hard-pressed Republic. The International Brigade was formed and impassioned youth from England, France, the USSR, the U.S. (Lincoln Battalion) and even German émigrés came to Spain to fight for the government. Most of the democratic press was on the side of the Loyalists as were many famous writers, including Ernest Hemingway, Ring Lardner, the Mann Brothers (Thomas and Heinrich), and André Malraux—to name a few.

Unfortunately, it was a lop-sided fight. The Republican Army was short on weapons and money, and had only a small Air Force at its disposal. Franco's Fascists, on the other hand, received the most modern weapons from Italy and Germany. The volunteers of the International Brigade fought with machine guns and hand grenades against tanks and airplanes. But they held their ground.

This was the first armed resistance against Fascism, and a victory in Spain would have sent a serious warning to Germany and Italy to stop their bellicose activities. It was a war I believed in and I wanted to do my part. I found a recruiting station for the

German Battalion (Thaelmann Brigade) in Lausanne and volunteered. "Too young, come back in six months" was the answer. It was a lucky break for me because despite heroic fighting for years, the Loyalists were overpowered and the war ended with the defeat of the Republic.

5

Early in 1939 I received a registered letter from my uncle who had emigrated to the U.S. It contained a one-way passage on the Cunard Line from Marseilles to Haifa and an official-looking document in English, Hebrew and Arabic, issued by the British Mandate Office. It gave permission for Walter Bodlander, a minor, to immigrate to Palestine under the visa issued to his mother.

Years earlier, in 1935, my parents had applied for a visa to the United States. At that time they were told that there would be a long waiting period. No one could foresee when that visa would be issued and up until that time, there had been no word from the U.S.

Meanwhile, my uncle had apparently succeeded in getting a visa for his sister and me for Palestine and, indeed, a few days later I received a note from my mother that she had just arrived in Jerusalem. I was expected to meet her there after my graduation. Now, Palestine was certainly not where I wanted to go, but the visa was an insurance policy, and Palestine a place to escape if absolutely necessary.

That June of 1939 I graduated from Ecole de Commerce. By early July I received the first official notification that my student visa had expired and I was to leave Switzerland. Meanwhile the relationship with Jeanette had become much more intense. We were deeply in love and saw each other almost daily. We went for long walks along the lake, talked about the future—the world's and ours—and in the evenings, we danced at the Rotonde. If ever a time was bittersweet, this was it. We were so in love but we both knew our relationship could end any moment. I was now staying illegally in Switzerland and I had no intention to go to Palestine. Certain that at any moment war would break out, I told Jeanette my plan to volunteer for the French Army. As the summer progressed, many an evening at the Rotonde ended in sadness as we promised to "wait" for each other—for at least three years.

By mid-August the local police gave me an ultimatum: "Leave or be extradited." The last time we danced at the Rotonde, I promised to write. Jeanette promised to wait and then I left. Two days later, August 23, I was on the train to Marseilles.

The years in Neuchatel had been good years. I enjoyed school where I had learned French Literature and History. French culture was so different and so much more appealing to me than the cold Prussian militaristic attitude under which I had been raised.

I loved everything French—the language, the songs, the writers and the philosophers who had brought us the Enlightenment. Malraux and Gide and other modern left-leaning writers were my favorites. My French became fluent and immaculate—no accent whatsoever. My grades were excellent. It was a compete reversal from my school experience in Germany where all learning had been a drudgery.

My friendships with Francois—the German Jewish colleague who also lived at Webers, and with Cyril, the Russian-Swiss student, had deepened. Those relationships actually lasted a lifetime. During those four years, we would meet frequently at the Café du Theatre, a local bistro, to discuss politics, or current events, literature, movies and the plays of the week. One of my idols was Sasha Guitry, the French Noel Coward. Witty, gifted, an amusing writer and actor, he had formed his own acting troupe and toured the French-speaking world, performing his plays.

When he came to Neuchatel we all went to see him and after the performance, we joined a large group of admirers at the artists' entrance of the theater, waiting for a glimpse of the great man. It was a November night and it had just started to snow. Finally the stage door, opened and Mr. Guitry appeared. He took in the scene of the adoring applauding crowd for a few seconds and then, ignoring us all, and with the most condescending tone, observed: "It's snowing, how nice."

And with that, he descended into his waiting car and disappeared. What he was really saying was: "How nice of you to make it snow for me. I'm glad you realize I appreciate it." Thus, another of my idols fell off his pedestal. I still thought he was very gifted and liked him until 1941 when I discovered he had collaborated with the Nazis. He was tried in France after the war, found guilty, and served time in prison.

At the end of the last semester, my French Literature professor asked me what my plans were after graduation. What did I intend to become? Actually, I had not given much thought about it and told him so. He told me that he had noted my ability to write good compositions and that he thought I should pursue a field allowing me to utilize my writing abilities. He mentioned journalism and film. Having left home at 15, no one had ever seriously discussed my professional ambitions or hopes with me. So I was much impressed that one of my teachers had taken such an interest in me.

We met several times on campus and when I graduated, he invited me to dinner at a very fancy restaurant. The dinner ended with cigars and cognac. His name was Pierre Borel. We became friends and, of course, he knew of my problem with the immigration authorities. I introduced him to Jeanette and the three of us had a number of wonderful evenings of wine and beer at the Café du Theatre.

He approved of our love affair and promised to look after her when I left. He came to the station that August 25 when I bordered the train for Marseilles. He was the only one there. Francois had already emigrated to Brazil, Cyril was on vacation visiting his mother in Bern, and Jeanette had absolutely refused to come. She and I had made our farewells the night before and as she had jumped out of my window into the courtyard she had turned and said: "Je t'aimerai toujours". Pierre asked me: "How much money do you have?" When I told him about 10 francs, he gave me 200 and said, "You can pay me back some day." Oh Pierre, much later I suspected you were a bit in love with me, although there was never the slightest sexual suggestion or impropriety.

Five or six years after the war, I received a package from Neuchatel. How did he find my address? The package contained a book, a novel by Pierre Borel and it had a printed dedication: "To Walter Bodlander: Across the oceans that separate us, I dedicate my first novel to you."

Well, Pierre, I never wrote you. I never wrote Jeanette. I never wrote a letter to anyone after I left Neuchatel. I never acknowledged the book and for many years I did not even read it. I could not deal with my past and, of course, you would only have been hurt by what must have seemed my obvious indifference. For years I dreamed of Jeanette, I wanted to write her, but to what address? The war years made it impossible and later it seemed futile. I finally buried it all in oblivion. So in a sense, our friendship was a victim of my love for Jeanette.

Years later, in the early 1960s, friends of mine were among the first Americans to travel to Europe. They were going to Switzerland and I prevailed upon them to stop in Neuchatel. I told them to look for Pierre Borel in the phone book. When they returned to Los Angeles, they told me that they actually had found him. They had gone to his home and when they rang his doorbell, a gentleman opened and said, "Yes, I'm Pierre Borel." They introduced themselves—friends of Walter Bodlander from Los Angeles—and explained they wanted to give him a message from Walter. The man responded: "Sorry I don't know such a person" and he closed the door.

Many years later, in the 1980s, while passing through Neuchatel, I tried to find Pierre. The local public library had several of his books, so I asked the librarian if she could help me find him. She was very accommodating and disappeared to do some research. She returned shortly. Mr. Pierre Borel had died in 1977.

6

In August 1939, when the Soviet Union signed the non-aggression pact with Hitler, most people on the political left—like me—were repelled and disgusted. It was considered a betrayal of Socialist principles. I saw it differently then—and still see it differently now.

Ever since the Revolution of 1917, the Soviet leaders had fostered a deep distrust of the Western World. And their skepticism was well founded. It was a fact that the Western powers had intervened militarily in the Russian Civil War. Allied armies had been fighting side by side with the Tsarist White army as late as 1920, hoping to overthrow the new communist government.

When this proved unsuccessful, it was also a fact that Western governments (with the exception of the weak and impotent German Weimar Republic) were inimical to the new Russia of the Soviet Union. True, they had cause.

The Comintern (Communist International Congress) established in 1919 by the Soviet government called for "communist world-wide revolutions, armed if necessary." Not exactly a political program designed to establish friendly relations with the West. But this view—primarily advocated by Trotsky—had been repudiated by Stalin in 1925. He now directed the Comintern to work for "Communism in One Country", namely the Soviet Union. Thus, after 1925, communist world revolution was no longer a goal of the USSR—a fact the West chose to ignore. Russia felt isolated and it was. Devastated after a lost war and a terrible peace treaty (Brest-Litovsk, 1918), impoverished by centuries of feudal rule, burdened by a population primarily agrarian and 90 percent illiterate; the new Soviet government had its hands full to join the 20th century.

When Nazi Germany began to rise and to rearm under the banner of anti-communism, the Soviet Union had good reason for alarm. When Hitler told his people and the world that he intended to destroy the evil Soviets once and for all and would then take the lands from the inferior Slavs and settle them with his beloved Arian Germans, they believed him. The slogan was: "Germany needs Lebensraum" in other words, "space to live in".

The USSR was not alone in believing Hitler. Many of the governing forces in France and England were inclined to believe him as well. To them, it seemed a splendid idea. Let the over-bearing Germans, now freely re-arming, turn against the horrid Russians. At best they would destroy each other in bloody battles. And were the Germans to win, as was anticipated, they would certainly be weakened from the bloodletting.

Besides, a fascist Germany was not the end of the world. Jewish influence in politics and finance would be severely curtailed—as well it should be—and eventual accommodation with a Nazi regime would certainly be possible.

Of course, that was not the official line. But it certainly explains the frustrating passivity of France and England and the U.S. as they watched the rapid re-arming of Germany. How else can one explain the silence of the West as German expansion marched resolutely from the military occupation of the west bank of the Rhine to the militarization of the Saar, the destruction of the democratic government of Spain, the Anschluss of Austria, the invasion of Albania by Germany's fascist ally Italy, the emasculation of Czechoslovakia and the eventual occupation of that unfortunate country. All this happened, not suddenly, but slowly and methodically.

During that period the Soviet Union warned that the fascist countries had to be stopped before they became too powerful. Foreign minister Litvinov implored the Western democracies month after month at the League of Nations to form a united front against aggression. "Collective Security" was the key word and collective security was given lip service by France and England but not a single agreement was made to stop German expansion. And as time went by in fruitless discussion, Germany became ever stronger.

Finally after years of failing to reach any agreement, the Soviet Union realized that the West had no intention of stopping the Nazis, as long as they moved in the right direction—East. And so in the hope of gaining time to rebuild his tattered Red Army and to prepare against a German invasion, Stalin—at the last moment—signed a Non-Aggression Pact with his most deadly enemy. It was a respite for the USSR and a golden opportunity for Hitler to avoid a two-front war. He was now free to attack France.

This then was the state of world affairs as I saw it that evening of August 25, 1939, as the train for Marseilles left Neuchatel. For months I knew I would have to leave Jeanette. I was prepared, but now it became stark reality. I was so in love. I knew she would not come to the station but I had hoped she might be there anyway. She wasn't.

When would I see her again, hold her, kiss her again? Would she wait? Waves of sadness, of love, of loneliness swept over me, but then, as the rhythmic rattle of the train reminded me of the present, these emotions gave way to enormous excitement.

Once again I was facing an uncertain future similar to the time I had first left Breslau. I was eagerly awaiting the challenges and mysteries that lay ahead. There was no doubt that war would begin before I set foot on a ship to Palestine. Hitler was now ready to invade Poland and this time I was certain the West could not back down. Now that I was almost 19, I was certain that the French Army would accept me.

The Spanish Civil War was over. Now came the real fight against the Nazis and I wanted to be part of it. But what if war were to break out that night before I reached France? Would they let me in? What if Hitler waited longer than I expected? How long could I stay in Marseilles if there was no war? Would Marseilles be bombed?

These and many other thoughts went through my head, and they actually helped to dampen the pain of missing Jeanette. I began to look around me. My compartment was completely empty. It was early evening—dark both outside and inside. The train, as was usual of all trains at that time, was in complete blackout. Windows were covered with black curtains and the compartment lights were low with a bluish tint.

At the French border there was a very long stop. An official came asking for passports. I gave him my British paper. Since it was in a language alien to him, he studied it at great length and finally, satisfied that the photo was indeed me, saluted and left. But the train did not. We stayed at the station for more than an hour. Finally, it began to slowly move on.

The trip to Marseilles lasted about four hours. We were expected to arrive about 10 p.m. Already it was past 9. The prospect of sitting in the dim compartment for hours on end made me nervous. I decided to walk through the train just to pass the time. No one had come aboard at the border and now as I walked from car to car I noticed that I was about the only passenger on this train of at least nine cars.

Finally, in one of the last cars, I saw a young woman my age, sitting alone. Of course, I stopped to talk to her. It turned out that our circumstances were remarkably similar. She had just finished school in Lausanne and was planning to join her parents in Palestine. Her name was Anna and she was pretty, teary, and frightened. Naturally, I invited her to come to my compartment and we decided to join forces.

The train stopped frequently in the middle of nowhere, and occasionally an official would come by to tell us that because of the worsening international situation, it was not certain that we would proceed to Marseilles. We did get there however, at 4 o'clock in the morning. We took our luggage and found a small hotel. Immediate problem: One room or two? Economics, of course, made me suggest one room and Anna agreed. Sharing accommodations with a girl was "a first" for me. We dropped our suitcases, dropped on the rather narrow bed and immediately fell asleep. We awoke early in the afternoon.

One of the first things we did was to call the Cunard Line to find out which ship was scheduled to go to Haifa and when. The answer was predictable: nothing was going anywhere until further notice. No passenger liner would venture into the Italian-dominated Mediterranean at this time. Please call back later.

"Anna," I said, "you should go back to Switzerland. With your brother there in residence, they will let you back in. This is clearly leading to war and when it comes, I will volunteer for the French army. What will you do here alone?"

"There is no war as I see it," she argued. "I want to stay and wait it out. In good time we will arrive in Palestine."

I had not mentioned Jeanette and, of course, I did not know for sure what would happen. Maybe, the Allies would give in again and let Hitler have Danzig. So I agreed and we stayed together.

We began to explore Marseilles and each other—the former with some success, the latter a complete failure. This is not the place to go into titillating details—the reader can find such in any modern novel. Suffice it to say that hormones easily won over guilt feelings about Jeanette. Since I was rather a novice in matters of sex, our clumsy union ended in Anna's frustrated and tearful exclamation: "Oh, why did we do this? And it wasn't even fun!"

Well, it was not so bad for me, but Jeanette was very much on my mind. Really, I thought, Anna should go back to Switzerland. During the next few days, the international situation became even more tense.

In Marseilles they began to build air raid shelters in public parks. That was quite a telling statement about French preparedness. German cities had been ready for war since 1936; here they began civil defense in the fall of 1939.

Four days had passed and we had seriously depleted our funds. Even Anna now saw the writing on the wall and with the few francs we had left, we bought her a ticket for Zurich. Her 1 p.m. train left at 4 a.m. on September 1, just hours before the war began. Immediately, trains to foreign countries were stopped. Anna found herself stranded without a cent—now an "Enemy Alien"—on a train to nowhere.

When I read the "extras" about the Polish invasion, I went back to the station to find out what might have happened to her train. No one knew. I then tried to call Anna's brother in Zurich but I did not have enough money for the call, and they would not accept reverse charges to a foreign country. Besides, they told me, all lines were busy.

Standing alone in that phone booth in Marseilles, I remember how aware I was of the historic importance of this moment. Today, I thought will be remembered forever. Hundreds of thousands of people will die because of what happened today.

Suddenly, I felt very lonely without Anna. By now it was almost noon. For a while I walked aimlessly through the streets. Then I went back to the hotel to give up our room. It was now time to volunteer for the army.

The enrollment station was at the Caserne Odeou on top of a hill overlooking the town. The little luggage I had, I left at the hotel and so, totally unencumbered, I headed toward my military destiny. By afternoon I stood before a sergeant offering my services to France. Around me—total turmoil.

General mobilization had been ordered a few days before and the number of men reporting for duty completely overwhelmed the military bureaucracy. I was given a short form to fill out, sent to the next room for shoes and uniform (shoes and trousers were available in my size, but there were no shirts and tunics) and, thus, clad partly in khaki and partly as a man of the military, I moved to the next station where I took the oath which made me an official French soldier. The next few days consisted of eating and waiting. The war news were exciting and reassuring.

England had declared war, the Poles were fighting valiantly and despite a few setbacks, the situation seemed to be under control. Neither Germany nor France had crossed each other's borders and there had been no air raids. The only aggressive action in the West was some minor artillery duels, causing no serious damage.

Soon I was assigned to an infantry unit for basic training, but not for long. Within four of five days, I was asked to report to my commanding officer.

"Bodlander," he said, "we seem to be missing some documents. We don't have a birth certificate nor a police residence report. Do you still have them? We need them."

For a moment I was tempted to lie but then lost my nerve and just stammered: "Hmm... well, hmm... Yes, you see," but then he interrupted me. "Where are you from anyway? Alsace or some place in the North? You sure as hell aren't from here (Midi)?"

"Well," I confessed, "I came from Switzerland, the French part—Neuchatel."

"So you are French. Where is your birth certificate?"

"Hmm... I'm actually not French; in fact, I'm not Swiss either. I'm stateless. I was born in Germany, but I'm not German. I'm stateless and Jewish."

There was a very long silence and then he said: "I have to call the commander. I can't deal with this."

That is how I found myself standing in front of a very genteel elderly General who kept shaking his head in disbelief.

"You mean they let you take the oath without any documentation? Well, we cannot keep you in the army. You have to be a French citizen. I can't believe this. We are so disorganized. Anyway, you must be mustered out immediately."

"But I want to fight for France and against the Nazis."

"Well," he said, "I can send you over to the Foreign Legion, they'll take you."

Now I had heard all kinds of horror stories about the Legion. Most of the soldiers were former criminals, fugitives from all over the world, crude and untrustworthy characters, mixed with a sprinkling of adventurous soldiers of fortune. Somehow I did not feel that I fit into that milieu. Also I had heard that the Legion was used by the regular army to do the most undesirable and dangerous tasks, such as clearing minefields. These were stories from books and movies of the time and though greatly exaggerated, I believed them. So I protested vigorously.

"I want to fight but in the regular French army, with my French comrades. I don't want to join the Legion."

We were at an impasse.

"You are, you know, an enemy alien. I'll have to send you to an internment camp." The General sighed, "Come on, join the legion."

"I have a visa to go to Palestine," I countered. "And I have passage, but there are no ships going through the Mediterranean at this time. Will you allow me to stay in the army until a ship arrives?"

"No," he said after some thought. "I'll tell you what: The police chief of Marseilles is a good friend of mine. I'll call him. You'll be allowed to stay in town until a passage to Palestine is available, but you must report to him twice a week and let him know where you are and what the status is of your impending departure."

Thus ended my glorious service in the French army. The police chief was friendly and pleasant and totally uninterested in the whole affair. I remember vaguely that I met him for a few minutes, then he deputized someone to whom I was to report by phone once a week. Nobody really cared.

7

It was now early afternoon and I decided to go back to my hotel hoping to negotiate some deal to stay, in return for everything in my suitcase. There was, however, a problem: my suitcase was gone and the manager made it clear that without money there would be no room.

Armed with my old expired German passport, the British paper allowing me entrance into Palestine and the ticket for Haifa, I began to walk the streets of Marseilles. September that year was unusually hot. I stopped at a cart where they sold lemonade for one centime a glass and then suddenly realized that I could not afford it: I had absolutely no money. It was a very strange feeling and, I thought, rather amusing.

I kept walking aimlessly and arrived at the beautiful broad avenue La Cannebière. The crowded sidewalk cafes were a new exotic experience for me. Neither Breslau nor Neuchatel had restaurants with tables right on the sidewalk interrupting the path and flow of pedestrians.

As I meandered through the crowd, wondering how I could get some food, a man asked me to sit at his table. Would I like a drink? I accepted but opted for coffee and a sandwich. I told him that I had no money to pay for it. No problem, he smiled. We began to talk about the war, but soon the topic changed. He was all alone, he lamented, and very lonely. At that point it occurred to me that the sandwich might have to be paid for with other than money, so I said that after I had eaten I would have to leave and if that was not agreeable, I would leave now. He was very pleasant, smiled and accepted my condition. That was my first meal as homeless.

Since I had no idea where I was going to stay that night, I went to the nearest police station for advice. From my accent they knew I was not from Marseilles and they laughed. And when I told them that I was not even French, they asked where I had come from.

"Then go to the Swiss Embassy," they said, and foolishly I took their advice. It was a long walk to the embassy and there, when they heard of my predicament, they laughed even harder than the police had.

"How can we help you? You're not Swiss. Good-bye."

Close by was a park. It was a warm evening so I spent that night and a few subsequent ones, outdoors. Each morning I would walk among the street cafes and use their restrooms to clean up. There was no shortage of homosexuals among the clientele and someone always bought me a meal accepting my conditions good-naturedly. Daily I went to the offices of the Cunard Line and always I heard the same answer: "Nothing has changed, we don't know if or when our liners will sail."

And every night I went back to my same spot in the park, which had become familiar and safe. I began to feel pretty smart—living off my wits. Occasionally, a man would insist on "payment" for a meal, but since all transactions were carried out in the busy populated street cafes, it was easy to get up and leave.

One morning as I was on my way from the park to the Cannebière, a young fellow stopped me to ask for a match. When I told him I did not have one, he gave me a cigarette and asked where I was going.

"Nowhere, especially," I replied.

"Well," he said, "I'm going swimming, would you like to come along?"

I had not had a shower for a few days, so the idea appealed.

"Sure, but I don't have any money and no bathing suit."

"No problem," he said. "I have extra trunks at my place. It's close by. We can pass there on the way."

So off we went. As we walked along, I realized we were getting into a part of town known as the Old Port. This is a section of Marseilles, not unlike the Kasbah of Algiers. Narrow streets end in courtyards, then resume again along stairs leading to other courtyards, then to a maze of walk-ways across narrow streets back into still another courtyard.

If one does not know the area, one is hopelessly lost and, in fact, years later, when the Nazis dominated Marseilles, the Resistance resided in the Old Part and could not be forced out until the police ordered the whole section destroyed. Anyway, I followed my guide until we entered a courtyard and there in front of a barn-like structure, he stopped and got out his keys to open a padlock.

"Here is where I live," he said. "Please hold this a minute." He gave me the lock. He opened the door, entered the dark barn and called me in. As soon as I entered, the door slammed shut and I stood in total darkness blinded by a flashlight the fellow was shining on me.

"Ok," he said, "empty your pockets and don't make a sound or I'll kill you."

A light hung from the ceiling and as he turned it on, I saw the knife in his hands. "Don't screw around," he warned, "tomorrow I report to the army and no one knows me around here. So let's have your money."

He must have been more frustrated than I was scared, if that is possible, when he realized that I had absolutely nothing of value on me. He took my watch, made me undress and searched every garment and finally—utterly annoyed—took his knife and made a cut across my arm.

"That's a warning," he said. "You go to the police, I'll finish the job."

Then he pushed me and my clothes into the yard and disappeared. Bleeding, scared, and completely lost, it took me well over an hour to find my way out of the Old Port into more familiar surroundings. This time they did not laugh at the police station. The cut was not serious and the bleeding had already stopped. Someone suggested I go to a refugee center. They gave me an address, almost at the other end of town, and gratefully I proceeded to walk there. The fun of my "Bohemian days" was gone. All there was left was fear.

I arrived at the refugee center a few hours later—exhausted and thirsty—only to find a note on the door that the center had moved to a new address. Once more, I walked across town. By late afternoon I finally arrived at the apartment house where the center was supposed to be headquartered but there was no answer at the door and not a soul in sight. By now my exhaustion had turned to defiance. I decided to sit in the courtyard and wait until someone would notice me.

By early evening a few people began to arrive—clearly they were refugees since they spoke German. But no one paid attention to me. Soon there were 20 or 30 people milling around the yard when someone asked for volunteers to help bring in the soup kettles. I immediately made myself available and, thus, met people who were in quite the same boat as I—stranded in France and without means. We brought soup and food from a kitchen nearby. Then I was introduced to one of the officials of the organization.

When he heard that I was German, he said: "Sorry, we can't help you, this is an Austrian Jewish Relief organization." I was speechless. A few people who had overheard the conversation became quite outraged and demanded an "emergency council" on my behalf, which resulted in a compromise allowing me to appear daily for food, but not for shelter.

Given my experience early that morning, I was terrified to sleep in the park. One fellow told me he, too, could only get food there and that he had pitched a tent on the lawn of the public library nearby with their permission as long as it would be taken down each day by 7 a.m. He offered to share it with me. I did not know if could trust him. I asked a few people if they knew him, they said: "Not really, but he had been around for some time and he seemed ok." Since I really had no choice, I accepted. Immediately after eating, we went to his tent. Everything was exactly as he had said it was. So after the first night, I felt totally safe.

Next morning we returned to the center for breakfast. My new friend suggested that I should earn some money. "You could sell newspapers and make enough to support yourself," he said. That's what he was doing. Well, in order to start such a business, one had to have about $5 to buy papers from the distribution center. He lent me the money and from that moment on I was financially independent.

Since we were still in the first weeks of the war, there were regular "Extra" editions of newspapers and business was brisk. The only trouble was buying the papers. These were still depression days. Men lined up to get their batch of papers to sell but the supply was limited. Often teenagers were shoved out of the line by older men. Clearly, I would have met with the same fate—or worse—had they known that I was not a local and not even French. So, despite my fluency in the language, I made a point never to open my mouth.

Now I had money to take the bus to report weekly to the police, and to go to the Cunard offices. From week to week there was little change in the international situation. Though everyone still expected Italy to join Germany, Mussolini made no move. This was the beginning of what journalists (and later, historians) called "the Phony War." The German army had overrun Poland in a few weeks, fighting had ended in the East. Along the German-French border, except for an occasional artillery duel, there was no hostile activity. No gas attacks, no aerial bombings. Europe was holding its breath. This paralysis also affected the Cunard line. No passenger ship dared to venture into the Mediterranean.

It was about mid-October. We had just lined up for lunch when someone called my name. The police station had phoned the Refugee Center. A French cruiser was leaving Marseilles for

Algiers and Lebanon. It would stop at Haifa on its way to let me off. I was to be on board by 2 p.m. That left about an hour and I could make it to the harbor on time but only if I took a taxi.

I said, "Forget it. I don't have the money. But someone ordered a taxi anyway. My fellow refugees instantly collected enough money for the driver. They pushed me into the car and off I went. We just barely made it. Thus, it came to pass that a French warship made an unscheduled stop at Haifa to let a Jewish refugee land. The ship's crew cheered as I left, regretting only that they did not get a leave on shore.

8

The city of Haifa leans up against Mount Carmel. When I arrived there in late 1939, it had distinct ethnic and commercial layers. On the harbor level were industrial yards, banks, international commercial firms and a major hotel to accommodate visiting businessmen. The hotel was also the place where the British army quartered their officers. The few people who had homes in the harbor district were Arab businessmen.

Then about a mile uphill from there was the Arab section. Small houses—often shacks—street vendors and markets crowded together, all connected by narrow walkways—frequently so steep—that roads gave way to stairs. The next level up was Jewish Haifa with European style houses and shops. This level included the government buildings, the famous Teknion, museums, theaters and movie houses along wide boulevards. This was the cultural center of the city.

Next up the mountain came a very wealthy Arab section with large beautiful estates. Finally, on top of Mount Carmel sprawled a residential area on which both Arabs and Jews resided. All these sections were connected by a wide highway winding its way from the harbor to the top of the mountain. A municipal bus service and numerous taxis provided transportation.

Few Jews ventured into the Arab or harbor areas at night and although the city was quite segregated, there were some Arab shops and coffee houses in the Jewish section. The British, mandated by the League of Nations to administer Palestine, preferred the Jewish sector. There the British were omnipresent and heavy handed. They patrolled the streets in twos and threes, swagger sticks in hand, pointing at girls or merchandise they wished to buy. Generally, they were heartily disliked. The only thing Arabs and Jews could agree upon was their contempt for the British.

For centuries, Palestinian Arabs and Jews had lived quietly and often in friendship together. In the early 1900s, as Jewish immigration began to increase there had been occasional fights resulting in casualties on both sides. The rise of Hitler gave impetus to the Zionist movement, which advocated a Jewish homeland in Palestine.

Beginning in the 1930s, the number of Jews immigrating to Palestine increased significantly. Census figures show that the Jewish population that had been about 3 percent before 1920 had risen to 30 percent by the time I arrived in 1939.

Arab leaders took a dim view of this increase and were determined to stop it. Zionist and later all Jewish relief organizations on the other hand pointed to Nazi atrocities in Europe and argued for the urgent need of an open immigration policy. The British overlords took the easiest way out by promising absolute support to both sides (Balfour Declaration for the Jews). By 1940 Jewish immigration permits were restricted to placate the Arabs.

Meanwhile Arab organizations took matters into their own hands and began to harass the Jewish population. Stabbings, occasionally fatal, were frequent, and often homemade bombs were thrown into busses known to pass through the Jewish sector. To allow for bus windows to be open, the glass panes had to be removed and replaced with chicken wire.

After a major attack by Arab youths in the Jewish quarter of Haifa in 1938, barbed wire had been strung to separate the two sectors. Only one walkway was left open. The highway was always open, but the last bus from the harbor to the Jewish sector left at 5 p.m., just before dusk. To drive this area at night was obviously not safe. These tense times were deemed "The Troubles"—not exactly war, but certainly not peace.

My mother had emigrated from Germany in November 1938, immediately following Chrystallnacht. Her brother had deposited sufficient money in her name to allow her—and me, her under-aged son—to enter Palestine under a "Capitalist Visa". Now she lived in a small apartment at the edge of Jerusalem in the suburb Kyrat Schmuel. I phoned her upon my arrival and she rushed to meet me. It was no doubt an emotional reunion for her since she had not heard from me after I had left Neuchatel.

Now she told me that my uncle had paid for my enrollment at the Teknion—the Jewish equivalent to MIT (Massachusetts Institute of Technology) or Cal Tech. In addition to the academic section, the Teknion also maintained a technical division where young people were trained in various trades. That is where I was enrolled. I was to be a blacksmith apprentice. This seemed to me to be the most preposterous idea. I had no interest to work in anything mechanical and I certainly was not going to become a blacksmith. Pierre Borel's suggestion that I should be a journalist was more of what I had in mind.

Why my uncle had thought of me as a future blacksmith is not quite clear to me—even today. True, during 1940 the Great Depression was still in full swing. He may have reasoned that in the U.S., where I would eventually end up, a trade rather than a profession would more likely lead to employment. That is how I could justify this strange decision, but it certainly pointed to the enormous gulf between him and me.

As a child and adolescent in Germany, I had dearly loved my uncle. He was my hero and my ideal. My immediate family was very small: father, mother and Uncle Ernest—my mother's brother. While we were financially "well off", my uncle was clearly very rich. We lived in a nine- room apartment in which I was told my grandparents had lived. It was an old place and located almost downtown. Uncle Ernest lived in a modern villa in the most fashionable part of Breslau.

He was a bachelor: "too busy to get married"—was his answer to persistent questions. He came to our apartment frequently, usually in the evening, after work. In those days the main meal was served at noon. Dinner was light: cold cuts, some cheeses for a sandwich, maybe an egg dish. This was Germany in the early 20s and food was still in short supply and expensive.

There I was: four years old—maybe five—when my uncle would stop by. "No, no," he'd protest. he did not want anything to eat. Meanwhile, in the process of discussing the political situation of the day, he would absentmindedly take a slice of bread, butter it heavily and pile high slices of sausages and cheeses making himself an open-faced sandwich. What daring, what style, what panache! My sandwich consisted of one thin slice of meat between two dry pieces of bread. No wonder I idolized him.

Most Sundays we would visit him at his place. He had an excellent cook, Fraulein Gertrud, who served the best-baked goose in Breslau. After lunch my father and uncle would light up their cigars and play chess and I was allowed to watch. To this day the smell of cigar smoke reminds me of those lazy quiet Sunday afternoons. Those were good times. I had complete freedom in his place. I knew where the candy was hidden and where to find interesting books.

Once in a while I was allowed to stay overnight. Then next morning, my uncle and I would have breakfast and that was when we talked: about my friends, my thoughts and aspirations, and later, about politics and economics. He formulated my desire to be as suave and generous as he was, and as fair and wise. Somehow, he overshadowed my father even though I loved and respected my father who to me was the kindest man I ever knew. But my father was close by every day; my uncle seemed special.

The only and, thus, the most memorable holiday we celebrated was Christmas. Today, I am not so sure I know what we were thinking. Of course, we did not celebrate the birth of Jesus and certainly not the birth of Christ, but since Christmas was a major event in Germany, we, as good assimilated Jews, joined the general population in celebration. And with gusto! Festivities began on December 23 with major housecleaning and baking. My mother rarely cooked but she loved to bake and make complicated deserts and she was very good at it. Wonderful smells permeated the house, promising exciting things to come. Christmas eve around 4 p.m.—just before it got dark outside—father's study, which had been closed to me during the day, was opened, and father, mother, our cook and I entered.

Awaiting us was a beautiful Christmas tree decorated with burning candles and edible goodies—chocolates, oranges, apples, and marzipan. Nuts wrapped in gold and silver foil hung from the branches and at the foot of the tree, beneath all this—the gifts.

Then, after much joyful unwrapping and excitement, we packed up and went to my uncle's place (without the cook). Here we were ushered into a waiting room together with my uncle's best friends Mr. and Mrs. Marcus until finally my uncle led us to his living room. There, lit only by the candles of the huge Christmas tree, which, of course, was even larger than ours at home, the room echoed with the sound of "Silent Night". It was a recording but everyone joined in the singing, especially Fraulein Gertrud, whose lovely soprano still rings in my ears.

Then the lights were turned on and everyone was directed to his or her own gift table. For me, the gifts were always the top of my list—the real big items—maybe a bicycle or a phonograph. Always there were additional unexpected surprises. It was heaven for a little boy. Once the unwrapping was done, we moved to the dining room for a lengthy and delicious feast at which I was permitted a glass of wine. Tired, excited though exhausted, I went to bed and stayed at my uncle's place for Christmas Day.

That was the man who now thought I should train to become a blacksmith. My mother could not contradict her brother and I cannot blame her. She had just been saved by his generosity. Without his money she would not have been able to leave Germany, let alone get a visa to Palestine. Our own money had virtually disappeared. The factory—well established for more than 80 years was in ever-increasing danger to be confiscated by the Nazis. So, in 1938, she had sold it to our accountants for the price of the inventory and the machinery. It was to be an installment sale. In reality, most of the money was never paid. Whatever money she did receive was used to get the exit permission from the German government.

First one had to pay the appropriate income taxes, then the hefty "Reich Flucht Steuer" (Fugitive Tax). The remaining money, which the government approved for taking out, had then to be exchanged into foreign currency at extremely unfavorable rates, established by the Nazi government. The usual result was that only a small percentage of the original money was left. In my mother's case: not enough to get a visa to anywhere.

This was one of the many reasons that so many Jews did not—or could not—leave Germany.

9

So there I was in Haifa. My mother had rented a small apartment for me close to the Teknion. "I cannot stay in Haifa," she told me. "I have a job in Jerusalem." Indeed, she had been hired by the Jerusalem YWCA as a cook. Knowing her skills in that department, I was not surprised that in short order a rebellion by the Y guests led to my mother's transfer from the kitchen to administration. Eventually, she became the manager of the Y facility.

Reluctant but obedient, I enrolled in the Teknion "Shops" department. An elderly but kind instructor handed me a file and a slab of iron and said: "File this. Make it level." I tried but failed. I tried again, the verdict: "no good". The teacher was amused by the utter ineptitude of this new "Jecke". A German Jew trying his hand at a trade! What a clumsy fool, he must have thought.

For me this was an introduction to the hierarchy of Jewish prejudice. "Jacke" was German for a "suit" or "jacket". The Yiddish version is "jecke" which is what German Jews in Palestine were called, presumably because many of the early German immigrants coming from middle class backgrounds had worn suits rather than work clothes.

They were on top of the totem pole because they were thought to be the best educated. They were also perceived as arrogant and, consequently, were disliked by all others. Next came the Russian Jews, who were among the early immigrants to

Palestine in the late 19th century, the pioneers, the workers and "kibutzniks". Then the Polish and Baltic Jews. At the bottom of the heap were the Levantine Jews from Spain and Arab countries. By the 1940s, a new class was emerging—proud and defiant—and, in their mind, "the best". They were the native-born Jews of Palestine, later Israel. They called themselves "Zabres" after the fruit of the native cactus. Prickly on the outside; sweet, inside. Sad to say, Jews are as prone to prejudice as others. We have not learned much from our painful experiences throughout the centuries.

My stay at the Teknion lasted two days. I returned the file and iron cube to my instructor and left.

Once, long ago, I had thought of working in the hotel business. So now, relieved of my blacksmith duties, I looked for a job and got hired as a waiter at the bar of the large English-owned and Arab-run hotel at the harbor. It was posh—the word for "fancy" at the time, and the predominant guests were British officers. Mandated by the League of Nations to govern Palestine, they behaved in the obnoxious manner of colonial masters.

My English was as bad as their German—in other words, non-existent—and so, most of the time they bellowed orders at me, which I did not understand. Fortunately, there was another German immigrant waiter and we became friends. He helped me and made me feel at home in this new and strange milieu.

I began learning a few English words and was soon rewarded by being promoted to "morning waiter". The job now was to bring breakfast trays to my colonial masters' rooms. This is how I first heard of the barbaric idea of eating meat for breakfast. In Germany and Switzerland, we ate eggs and toast, but here the Brits were used to ham and bacon with their eggs. Also new to me were cornflakes (small bits of stuff tasting like cardboard) and kippers (smoked fish unfit for civilized breakfasts).

After a few months I got a raise and a new assignment: Afternoon bartender. It was exciting for me, particularly since I knew nothing about cocktails, which, in addition to beer was what Brits ordered most.

Again, I was rescued by my German friend who gave me a recipe book, which contained the basic mixtures.

From my apartment on Herzl Street in the Jewish sector, I took the bus daily to the harbor and returned on the last bus in the afternoon. Occasionally, I missed it. Walking home on the well-lit bus road would have taken a very long time. So I used to take the much shorter narrow walkways up through the Arab section. Paths, stairs, more paths, a turn to the left, up two steps and a sharp right. It was a labyrinth but one could not go very wrong because the main idea was to go uphill.

There was, however, one major problem: most roads between the Arab and Jewish sections led to dead ends—closed by barbed wire barricades. Only one remained open. I had learned how to find my way and as long as there was still daylight, I felt it was not too dangerous to risk the shortcut.

The spring and summer of 1940 was disastrous for the Allies. Holland, Belgium and France had all had been defeated and the British Army had been thrown out of Europe. The Empire needed help. In Palestine, it did not get it from the Jewish population.

By the time I arrived in Haifa, there had been a number of Jewish protests brought on by the British refusal to allow refugees from Europe to immigrate. It was a strange and rather absurd situation for many of us. Here England was fighting against the most vicious enemy of the Jews—virtually alone and nearly beaten—and we, Jews, were in the streets protesting against that same England for not helping the most helpless.

But for England to give sanctuary to the refugees meant to alienate the Arabs of the Middle East. With German armies at the doors of Egypt, it is very understandable that they would do anything to appease the Arabs, especially since most recently the religious leader of the Palestinian Moslems, the Grand Mufti of Jerusalem, had issued a proclamation in which he praised Hitler and urged his Moslem followers to sabotage the British war effort.

By then, the Palestinian Jewish population was strongly anti-British but seriously divided about how to achieve the common aim—the Jewish Homeland. On one side, and by far in the majority, were the Histadrut and the Haganah—a coalition of labor unions, kibbutzim, and left-wing political parties.

They hoped to make deals with the British—to persuade them that humanitarian considerations were important. Their main weapon was civil disobedience and they were willing to use economic pressure to make British life in Palestine uncomfortable. When a ship of refugees was known to be sailing for Haifa and had not received permission to dock, they called for demonstrations and boycotts.

In the Jewish sections of the city, all shops closed, sometimes for days. All restaurants and coffee shops were locked up. Movies and theaters stopped performances. Thousands marched in the streets and obstructed entrance to public offices. During these strikes, civic government came to a halt. The army hated these protests. Instead of shopping and relaxing in the Jewish sector, they were now forced to patrol the streets. Usually the Brits ordered a curfew. Everyone had to be indoors by nightfall. No one obeyed it. Occasionally, there were clashes between soldiers and protestors but rarely was there serious violence.

Very different was the tactic of the Jewish "right", which was split into two main groups: one was known as the Stern Gang; the other, as the Jabotinsky Group. These groups were extremists; they considered the British the enemy, and they were intent on using violence to achieve their goals. They were terrorists and proud of it. They bombed hotels where British troops were stationed, most notably the King David Hotel in Jerusalem, and they tortured and hanged British soldiers if they succeeded in capturing them. Their activities led to many innocent civilian deaths. In my opinion, they were as fanatic and unreasonable as the Nazis. I despised them and had nothing to do with them. They were a loud minority and, sadly, some of them later became prominent leaders in Israel.

Once in a while, working at the hotel, I would miss the last bus and have to walk home through the Arab sector but that had always happened in daylight. Then came a day when I totally miscalculated. It was much later than I thought and as I left work and climbed up through the Arab sector, it became dark. There were no streetlights. Outside their houses, Arab men sat and relaxed and smiled in surprise at a lone Jew passing by. Now I was sure someone was sneaking up on me. So I walked faster and, of course, lost my way.

Finally, I made it to the top, to the Jewish sector—only to be stopped by the barbed wire barricade. Panicked, I turned around. An old Arab, who had watched my dilemma, motioned to me to go to my right and then uphill. But was this a trap to kill me or was it a friendly tip? You guess. By the time I got home I was exhausted, frightened and relieved. I swore I would never do that again—but when one is 20, such resolutions never last forever. Just before I left Palestine, I did something quite similar but even more foolish.

10

Those days in Haifa were very lonely ones. My thoughts were constantly with Jeanette—but how to contact her? She, of course, had no idea where I was, and since Europe was now at war, I was sure no letter would get to Pierre even if I were to write. But there was something else. Feeling so isolated, so lost, so without plan or purpose, I was worried that my letters would be nothing but tearful complaints—certainly not the best tone for love letters. So, no letters were written and none received by my friends in Neuchatel.

There were, of course, young people around and I met some of them by becoming involved in the political activities of the left. It was already fashionable to speak Ivrit—Modern Hebrew. Since I had no intention of staying in Palestine I stubbornly refused to learn the language. Not a very smart decision, I might add, since it became "de rigueur" at least to learn, if not to speak Ivrit if one wanted to get anything but a menial job. Since my friends and acquaintances were all refugees who spoke German I did not need the new 'native' Ivrit.

This rather dull life was spiced by the occasional calls for a strike to protest against the British refusal to allow yet another refugee ship to land. My work at the hotel also helped to solidify my dislike for Brits. Not once, in the eight months of room service and bar duty did any of the officers speak to me other than to give an order. Rarely did I hear a "Thank you".

In November 1940 a refugee ship, the Patria, sailed from Greece for Haifa. As usual it was denied a docking permit. It had been at sea for more than a week and then, in sight of the Haifa harbor, it had cabled that it was overloaded and about to run out of food and water. The British ordered it to sail for Mauritius. "Impossible," replied the captain. The ship is no longer seaworthy. He demanded immediate permission to dock.

The British stayed put and so did the Patria with its 1800 refugees—a mile out at sea and quite visible from shore. A strike was called. On the second day the demonstrations turned violent when it became known that the conditions on the Patria were rapidly deteriorating .The temperature was in the 90s and the ship was running low on water and there was no air conditioning on board. Of course I participated in the protest.

Thousands of us were marching to the Court House when the Brits began to use water cannons to disperse the crowd. At that point a number of the protesters threw "Molotov Cocktails" at the building and succeeded to set it afire. By then the Brits were really furious. They used their batons mercilessly and a good number of us ended in the hospital. Luckily, I got away unscathed.

On the morning of the third day, the British gave in and allowed the Patria into the harbor. But no one was permitted to leave the ship. Negotiations continued. It was about noon, I was at work, when I heard screams from hotel guests. I rushed to the window to see the Patria lean to one side and sink. It capsized in less than 15 minutes. More than 170 of the 1800 passengers died that day in Haifa harbor. No one knew what had caused the disaster.

Years later a book revealed that the Haganah had planted a bomb on board to dismantle the ship so that it could not possibly leave Haifa. A terrible miscalculation had sunk it. Eventually, the refugees who survived were allowed to stay in Palestine.

About that time I heard that defeated France had given rise to a resistance movement, which by then—under the leadership of General De Gaulle—was becoming a meaningful force in North Africa. Thousands of Frenchmen had escaped from their country and joined this new army, determined to continue the fight against the Nazis. Called the Free French, they were building an Air Force in Egypt and looking for volunteers. Nationality was no problem. Everyone was welcome. So I immediately filed the necessary papers and was told that shortly I would get a reply.

It had been sometime in 1935 that my parents had applied for a visa to the United States. There was, of course, a waiting list and they had been told that they would be notified when their name was reached. Five years later—about two months before the Patria affair—a letter had arrived at my mother's address in Jerusalem, stating that her son Walter would receive his U.S. Visa in several weeks. The problem was, what did "several" mean? How long was "several"?

A rush to the dictionary did not help and those who spoke English weren't sure. I called the U.S. Consulate and they simply confirmed that a visa would soon be issued to me, but not to my mother. No date, no explanation. Now more than two months had passed with no news. Meanwhile, my mother was trying to find a passage for me from Jerusalem to New York. I'm sure she called every available travel agency but since it was wartime, no passenger lines were crossing the Mediterranean, much less the Atlantic. It was then mid-November.

In anticipation of the Visa, I had quit the job at the hotel and moved to my mother's place in Jerusalem. I had made some friends there and one evening we all got together for a few beers. We were three couples. My partner was a pretty Polish girl, who spoke excellent German. We all got along famously. We were sitting in a garden café on the outskirts of town.

It was a moonlit night, balmy and fragrant with the smell of the warm earth and trees .The conversation was light and slightly alcoholic, the topics: love, politics, more love and adventure. Someone mentioned my birthday coming up in a few days and someone else said: "Let's celebrate tonight with a ride to the Dead Sea."

That seemed like a great idea. It was only 11 p.m., and we could easily be back by 3 or 4 in the morning. Everyone began to talk at once. Plans, ideas, suggestions were thrown around and after a few more beers only two problems remained. One was that The Dead Sea and the road to it was in Arab territory. That meant extreme adventure because we were at the height of "troubles" between Jews and Arabs.

Bombings and stabbings were in the news every day and we all were aware of the danger. The other problem was transportation. None of us had a car. Then someone said: "I know a taxi driver who will take us." By then, one could not really object. So we dispatched our genius to the phone and soon he came back. His "friend" would be ready in half an hour and the price—an affordable 10 pounds.

The taxi turned out to be a small truck with seats welded onto the flatbed. The driver was an Arab and we six passengers were by then rather silent and subdued. But beer, youth and moonlight soon changed the mood and as we left the lights of Jerusalem behind, we sang and joked in excited anticipation of a midnight swim without the benefit of bathing suits. I had never been to the Dead Sea and enjoyed the winding rocky road through this rough moonlit desert land. No one said a word when the driver stopped briefly at an Arab village "to tell his wife that he would be home late," as he told us.

We arrived at the shore in good time, found an easy access to the sea, and while we were swimming and frolicking in the water, the driver left with the truck to find a place to turn it around. The water was warm and buoyant and extremely salty. No one swam far and soon everyone got out. Although the air was calm and soft, we were rather cold and since we had no towels we began to run around the rocky shore, hoping to dry off faster.

Still wet, we got dressed—a group of happy innocent youngsters. Just then, as if by secret signal, the truck arrived, we got on and began the climb back to Jerusalem. By then, it was about two a.m. and we were exhausted and silent. Most of us slept or swayed drowsily in our seats, leaning against our neighbors.

I woke up when I realized that the truck was slowing. As I looked beyond the driver's cab, I saw in the distance a group of men blocking the road. We were approaching slowly, everyone by then was awake and aware of the ambush.

By the time the truck's headlights reached the menacing group, it turned out to be a bunch of oil drums left standing in the middle of the narrow road. We had no choice. Silently, we jumped down off the truck and rolled the stone-filled drums to the shoulder of the road. We all assumed that any moment the shooting would begin. Instead, total silence.

As we climbed back on the truck, the driver started up the engine and we were off again. We arrived in Jerusalem at about four o'clock in the morning. We paid the driver and went home— tired, excited, jubilant and frightened. I, for one, had been very scared. I slept almost the whole day and never told my mother where I had spent the night. A few days later "The Jerusalem Post" reported that five Jewish students on their way to the Dead Sea had been killed in an ambush.

11

A week after that experience, my U.S. Visa arrived and so did a letter from the Free French Army in Cairo, stating that, if physically fit, I would be accepted for service. I was to report within two weeks.

Now I was faced with a momentous decision, but I must admit: the choice was rather easy. Much as I had wanted to join the fight against Hitler, the opportunity to see the United States easily won the day, and when my mother found a passage across the ocean on an Egyptian merchant ship, the ZamZam, the voyage to the U.S. was a done deal. Suitcase in hand, I faced a tearful mother once again at a train station, this time on my way to Egypt. And once again, I felt the elation of freedom and escape.

It was the beginning of a journey into the future—alone, unafraid and armed with $100 (today's value), which was more money than I would ever need for the trip. The train brought me through the Sinai Desert to Port Said where a taxi took me to the harbor. It was about 8 p.m., as the trip from Jerusalem had taken all day. Although Port Said was alluringly exotic and exciting, it seemed a bad idea to explore the seedy harbor town at dusk, especially since the ZamZam was to sail so soon. So, on the evening of December 17, 1940, I reported to the ship's purser and was assigned my cabin. Intended for two, the room was extremely small, just enough space for double-decker bunk beds, a washbasin, a toilet, and a tiny table with an uncomfortable chair. I threw my suitcase on the upper bunk and finding myself exhausted, I lay down and fell asleep.

Next morning I awoke quite early. It was daylight and I was anxious to explore my new home. The ZamZam was a 10,000-ton passenger freighter, flying the Egyptian flag. That made it neutral except that the Germans might consider it British and, thus, a fair target. In addition to the cabins for about 100 passengers, it had a lounge with a small bar and tiny dance floor, a dining room, a den-like game room and a small but very useful library stacked with books in English, French and Arabic. Everything was on one level (crew cabins were below) and every room had access to the spacious deck, the entire length of the ship.

Wandering through the new surroundings, I passed the bar. A British or American clergyman was sitting there and when he spotted me, he said, "Good morning, fellow passenger. Sit down. Have a drink." Now here was an adventure. A respectable stranger offering me a drink. I was impressed and, of course, accepted. But, what does one drink before breakfast?

When the parson realized my dilemma, he suggested a Bloody Mary. Since he spoke only English, we struggled to get a conversation going. Soon it was my turn to offer a drink, and by that time my head was reeling and I was ready for food. I summoned the bartender, a burly Egyptian wearing a red fez, to pay my bill. "No need for cash," he said. "Here, just sign this note." This was my introduction to the idea of credit and I thought it was a splendid invention.

The ZamZam was scheduled to leave Port Said the night we went on board, but we were lucky, the ship did not leave until the following morning. Thus, we all stood on deck and watched the slow passage through the Suez Canal into the Red Sea. The canal is quite narrow and we could see the Egyptian farmers working their fields, watching us and waving. There were approximately 90 passengers aboard. It was interesting that people seemed reluctant to intermingle. Birds of feather... Almost immediately, the passengers divided into tightly knit groups. The largest consisted of some 30 middle-aged orthodox rabbis and their families. They either had been visiting Palestine and were now returning to the U.S., or they were immigrants to the New World. I had no occasion to speak to any of them except for a few teen-agers who had managed to escape their restrictive parents.

Next was a group of French-speaking passengers. The nucleus of that group was the band. A five men combo from Marseilles who had been stranded in Egypt, they were now on their way to Brazil for an extended gig in Rio. They played nightly for the ZamZam passengers. Most of them were accompanied by wives or girl friends. They were a loud, boisterous and genial group, joined by a number of Lebanese students who all spoke French. The remaining passengers were English-speaking, most of them American missionaries returning home.

Our first stop was to be Mombasa, the main port of Kenya. Then we were to sail along the east coast of Africa, pass between Madagascar and the main land, and then stop again at Cape Town, South Africa. From there, sailing around the Cape of Good Hope, the perilous trip across the South Atlantic was to bring us to Recife, Brazil. Then we were to sail slowly and carefully to Trinidad for a four-day stay, and finally to proceed along the North American coast, passing Cape Hatteras, to New York and then to Boston. The trip was expected to take about three and a half months.

Since the captain did not know how the Germans felt about an Egyptian ship filled with Jews, it was assumed that they would try to sink us. Thus, the strictest blackout rules were enforced. Every door to the deck and every porthole and window had two blackout curtains to assure that no light would escape. Smoking outside after dark was prohibited. The implied danger and the knowledge that the trip would take a very long time created an atmosphere of excitement and carefree enthusiasm among us younger passengers.

After the first week, rumors already began circulating among the younger bunch about who was sleeping with whom and if not, why not. As danger was in the air, so was sex—thick, fragrant and mysterious. It is however safe to say that wishful thinking, assisted by a vivid imagination lay at the bottom of most stories. In reality, there were light-hearted love affairs, flirtatious, exciting and—more often than not—unconsumed.

Within a few days some 20 of us youth knew each other, formed cliques and sub-cliques and generally behaved rather obnoxiously. The clique I belonged to called itself "Les Bleus". We were all French speaking and considered ourselves to be the "chosen elite". Blue, white and red are the French colors. "Les Blanks" had sounded racist. "Les Rouges", too political, so it was "Les Bleus." "Vive Les Bleus!" was our cry and since it had no meaning whatsoever, we thought it was rather humorous.

The remaining passengers had no idea why we were running around convulsed with laughter, shouting "Vive les Bleus" and the more they seemed to dislike us, the better we liked it. The band with their wives and /or girlfriends and Claire Marie, the ship's nurse were part of our "club". Other groups of young people were formed but since they spoke only English, communications with them was awkward.

I liked Claire Marie and I think she liked me. We began to hang out together. She was no threat to Jeanette but I became aware that my future with my Swiss sweetheart became more and more obscure. Thus, virtuous adherence to my already somewhat damaged vows to Jeanette stood in constant conflict with my adolescent desires. When Claire Marie rejected my too intense advances, I called her "Sainte Marie", and "Sainte Marie" it was, basically until the end of the trip. She liked her nickname and took great pleasure earning it ever so often.

There is not very much to do on a small ship, day after day. We were on the open ocean most of the time and although it was usually very hot, the deck that went all around the ship was the place to be. Les Bleus had appropriated a section at the front of the ship. Among the passengers, there was a group who had chosen to make it their job to keep a watch out for German submarines. They actually had constructed an elevated stand and this was constantly manned, probably to the silent amusement of the crew who, of course, had their own lookout.

At least two or three times a week these "hawks"—as we called them—insisted that they had spotted suspicious objects in the distance. Nervous and jittery, most passengers came out to take a look. There was much excitement, outstretched hands directed eyes to—what? A lot of ocean. Eventually, as the ZamZam plodded along, the excitement began to wane. Personally, I never did see anything, but many times others insisted that there was, indeed, some object in the distance.

The daily routine was to find a deck chair in a shady area and, with drink in hand, to read a book borrowed from the library. Flying fish provided the daytime entertainment—plentiful and always fascinating. The nights during good weather were spectacular, particularly when the moon was low. Looking at the endless and mysterious star-filled sky for hours was an unforgettable experience.

Claire Marie was usually on duty at the infirmary between 9 and 11 p.m. So these became my stargazing hours. The ZamZam had set its clocks so that daytime began at 6 o'clock and evening was around 7 p.m. As the ship cut across the ocean, it produced a phosphorous green white wash visible at night—a most hypnotic spectacle.

And then there were the parties. Almost daily in the afternoon "Les Bleus" would gather in the lounge for drinks, small talk and parlor games. In the evenings, the band would play and there would be dancing and drinking until 2 a.m. None of our group were alcoholics but the booze flowed freely and ever so often it was my turn to treat. With my newly found credit—that was no problem at all. I just signed the chits and joined the fun.

These were strange days, indeed, sometimes uneventful but always loaded with anticipation. What would tomorrow bring? So many new places to see, so much possible danger on the horizon. The unknown future in the U.S., the constant U-Boat menace, all these possibilities gave every moment an almost surrealistic intensity.

I'm sure these feelings were universal since despite the real possibility of a fatal enemy attack at any moment, none of the passengers showed any fear. We lived our life in fatalistic abandonment.

The band leader's wife took a shine to me. It lasted a few days and never went beyond a furtive kiss. One of the English girls wanted to crash our clique but she didn't succeed. I fell in love with Claire Marie. I was envious of every guy connected to a pretty girl. I cried for Jeanette. Every day, every hour stood on its own, my mood changed constantly, and the ZamZam sailed on as we made our first stop at Mombasa.

The entrance to this largest port of Kenya leads through a very long and narrow channel. The jungle on both sides is dense and romantic. I expected lions and elephants, but there was no wild life in sight, just beautiful and exotic landscape. We anchored outside the large harbor in the late afternoon. After about an hour, we were notified that those who wanted to go ashore could do so and have dinner at the hotel. About 30 passengers took advantage of the offer—all Les Bleus among them. We took a dingy ashore and a bus to the hotel.

Kenya was a British colony so why the hotel prepared a "Rijsttafel" I don't know. The meal is a Dutch-Indonesian feast consisting of rice and an endless array of wonderful fish, meat and vegetable dishes, each served in small portions on separate plates. We sat at a large banquet table, the 30 of us, each served by our own personal waiter. Red wine, white wine, pink wine flowed, every dish with the appropriate beverage. It was a perfect example of how colonial masters lived and the whole affair took several hours.

An announcement informed us that the dingy would take us back to the ZamZam at 1 a.m. As the meal ended, Claire Marie and I decided to take a stroll on the beach. Walking along the lagoon, we were intoxicated by the balmy equatorial night, the moon—nearly full—glistening in the water and the whisper of waves lapping lazily at the shore. It seemed the most natural thing to do. Naked, we jumped into the water.

Thus, for the second time in just a few months, I experienced a midnight swim. The sight of Claire Marie's body shimmering with watery diamonds in the moonlight was one of the most exciting and esthetically beautiful experiences of my innocent life. We embraced laughing at our daring exploit and, wet as we were, got dressed. Claire Marie put a kerchief, previously used as an adornment, over her wet hair and hand-in-hand we walked back to our group. No one seemed to have noticed our absence. Soon we boarded the dingy and this delightful episode, now ended, was never mentioned again. It became our silent secret.

Time and the ZamZam moved on rather listlessly. Two and a half weeks went by. Monotony set in and the few U-boat sightings, all unconfirmed, were more welcome distractions than frightening episodes. We passed through the Straits of Madagascar and finally anchored at Cape Town. We were, of course, anxious to go ashore and to explore this fabled part of the world, particularly since we would be staying for five days.

The Table Mountain in the distance and the city climbing toward it looked invitingly seductive. One can imagine the disappointment when it was announced that no Jewish passengers were allowed to disembark. The Smut government of South Africa, adamantly anti-Semitic—had taken the position that given the international situation, Jews were more likely to stay in the country illegally than other passengers.

This specious argument was accepted without protest and that was the end of my association with Les Bleus. They went ashore happily, leaving me behind. Claire Marie had the luxury of not having to make a decision. She was on duty and had to stay at the infirmary.

few passengers left the ship. Cape Town was their final destination. A number of new passengers came onboard, among them Goetz and Lucy Mayer and their young daughter Marianne. The Mayers were German Jews, about 10 years older than I. As we became acquainted, I liked them more and more, and eventually we became very good friends. As the ZamZam left Cape Town and began its long and most perilous journey, across the South Atlantic, Lucy told me her story. It was so remarkable that I retell it here.

I (Lucy) was at the University of Vienna as a graduate student in psychology when I met Fritz, a most stunning medical intern from Germany. We both were very busy with our work but a chance meeting at a New Year's Eve party, given by mutual friends, led to an intense romance. The following year when Fritz had finished his internship, he asked me to go with him to Hirschberg (Germany) where his family lived and where he intended to begin practice. We married in 1933—the year Hitler took power. Both my parents had died when I was a teenager and as an only child, my intense need to belong to a family added to the allure of being married. Fritz was immediately successful. Hirschberg, a small town at the foot of the Sudeten Mountains, was an idyllic resort—easy going, slow and friendly.

Fritz had lost his father shortly after our marriage, and his mother who really never warmed to me, decided to move to Berlin. There were few family doctors in town and it did not take long to build a nice comfortable practice. Marianne was born on May 5th. She was 14 months old when on July 12, 1933, as we sat down for dinner, a knock came at the door. I answered: three SA men (Sturmabteilung—which means "storm troopers") politely kicked their heels together. "Heil Hitler! Herr doctor is wanted at the City Hall."

"We're just having dinner," I replied. "He can be there in an hour."

"No, it's rather urgent."

By then, Fritz had come to the door. "I'll just get my jacket."

"Not necessary," said the SA men, "this will take no time at all. You'll be back shortly. We have a car here and we must leave right away." As they left, Fritz waved, and I heard him ask: "What's this all about?"

I remember waiting and eating some of the cold cuts we were having for dinner. As time went on, I became more and more nervous. Around 9 p.m., I decided to phone City Hall. Of course, no one answered. A call to the police got a laconic: "We have no information." The local hospital had not admitted anyone by his name. Reluctantly, I called SA headquarters. Their answer was short. "The Jew Kleinmann is not here." With that, they hung up.

After a sleepless night, I went to the police. They had heard of shootings in the night but could give me no details. Those came as I got home. An SA man was waiting for me. "Dr. Kleinmann and five other Jews who had been picked up for questioning last night were shot while attempting to flee. You can pick up the body of your husband at the morgue."

Hannah, my mother-in-law, came from Berlin to help with the baby. A police inquiry into the shooting was launched but got nowhere. Many friends came to help while I walked around in a dazed stupor. I told Hannah that I wanted to sell the house and move into a small apartment. "Absolutely not," she said. "We'll keep the house. I'll pay the mortgage."

In fact it became clear that she wanted to keep everything belonging to Fritz intact. When I told her that Marianne and I must leave Germany as soon as possible, that I could not stay there, she replied: "Now that's nonsense. Where would you go and how would you live? You're in shock and can't think rationally."

The stress of the situation added to the coldness between us. Fritz's death had widened the gulf. One evening, at dinner, Hannah said, "This would never have happened if Fritz had not belonged to the Party. You know that he joined only to impress you."

I was stunned. In fact Fritz had told me years earlier that he had intended to join the Communist Party because they were the most effective force to fight the Nazis. Although we frequently had discussed politics, that particular subject took no time at all. "Well, good," I had said. "You know that I've been a member for years." I told Hannah: "Fritz has been a Socialist before we met. He joined the Party as a symbolic gesture. To fight the Nazis, not to impress me."

She responded with icy, angry silence. It was at that moment that I realized it was better for Marianne to live with me alone in an empty, sad house rather than to live among two angry hurt adults. I thanked Hannah for her help, told her that I no longer needed it, and suggested she should return to Berlin. She agreed, but added: "I'll close my affairs there and then come back. We'll help each other."

During the next few months I received a number of threats both by mail and telephone. Usually they were vague: "You're next." Or "One less Jew makes a better country." But as the months passed, they became more specific. One of the last ones was: "Your time is running out."

Most of my Jewish friends were discussing the need to leave the country. There was, of course, a great division of opinion. Besides, even if one wanted to leave, the obstacles seemed too enormous to overcome. I thought it would be easier and wiser to stay and wait out this crazy, dangerous regime, which most of us hoped would soon be toppled. My Party friends—now, of course, underground—were wonderfully helpful during those months and all of them urged me to begin work to emigrate.

The days dragged on endlessly in fear, anxiety and concerns. Suddenly, I realized that many months had passed since Fritz's assassination and I was still paralyzed, unable to do anything. Then, in early 1936, a man knocked at my door, small suitcase in hand, and asked to come in for a brief question. He said he was a friend of X, a colleague of mine from university days and so I let him in.

He was a man of average height, average weight, about my age and with the kindest face I had ever seen. His smile seemed amused while at the same time, sad. I'm Goetz Mayer," he introduced himself, "from Vienna, where I was residing until recently in a leading position of the Communist Party. We have a number of mutual acquaintances and I'm sure you will want to check me out."

We were still standing by the door.

"Maybe we could sit down," he suggested. "What I have to say may take a while."

We went into the living room. I offered coffee and he gladly accepted. "Just black, no cream or sugar." "Actually," Goetz continued, "it would probably be best if you were to call a few of your friends from the Party to authenticate me, because what I have to say is rather important and you need to trust me."

I made three calls: two local. Both people knew Goetz by name. One knew him personally and described him correctly. Then I called Vienna, which took a while and when my friend there heard why I called, he just said: "I know, listen to him and I hope you will take his advice. Good luck, there is very little time." And he hung up.

I was getting very nervous. "Go ahead," I said.

"Well, Lucy," he began, "let me start by saying that I know a lot about you. I know, of course, of Fritz's murder. I know of your child and how old she is. I know of your mother-in-law and I know of your financial situation. I also know of your social situation and that's why I am here. The SA is about to arrest you and put you into protective custody. You will be sent to Dachau for an undetermined time. We are certain that this will happen in the next few days. You must leave Germany immediately and we know you have no place to go. I have an Austrian passport and an entrance visa to France for me, my wife and daughter." He paused for a moment. "I have no wife and daughter—yet."

He stopped talking and drank some coffee. I was totally stunned. The only noise came from the bedroom where Marianne had just awakened. Then Goetz went on "I'm here to marry you. That will give you Austrian citizenship. Your German passport, our marriage certificate, and my Austrian passport will hopefully get us across the German border. We will pass as honeymooners. France will give us no problem."

He pause, then added: "You and Maryanne are in grave danger. I hope you understand. It goes without saying that the marriage is pro forma and that I will not take advantage of it in any way."

I was completely bewildered. Wild emotions surged in me. I felt tears coming and then I began to laugh hysterically. This is like a melodramatic movie I thought. But I also knew I had to pull myself together and somehow respond intelligently.

"I hope you don't mind if I think about it for awhile. I'll call you next week. God, I don't even know you, do you have a phone number?"

I got up and brought some more coffee from the kitchen. "You know, this is crazy even to consider. And how do you know what the Nazis are planning?"

I was still trying to stop laughing or crying when Goetz interrupted: "Lucy, sit down, I know this sounds crazy but we live in a very crazy and dangerous world, and you of all people should be aware of it. The Party has pretty good intelligence and they are concerned about you. After all, you held an important position not so long ago. We should leave and we should leave today. We cannot get married here; you are too well known. I have a marriage permit arranged in Berlin. There's a train leaving here at

5:00 p.m. So you have two hours to think about it and 15 minutes to pack. Take a small suitcase, pack for you and Marianne, just clothes, no pictures or documents, which might tip off the Border Control that you are not returning. Call a few local friends and tell them you are going on a short vacation. Leave the house as if you were to return soon. And Lucy, stop crying. This is a very fortunate chance to outwit the Nazis."

I just sat there and then after a while, things began to sink in and with that, thousands of questions came flooding: What about money? How will we live? And you said something about France, how are we to cross the frontier without entry permits? Where in France are we going and how can we live there? On what? For how long? I don't speak a word of French.

Goetz got up and started pacing the floor. "Look Lucy," he said, "we will have lots of time to talk about the future. Right now you need to act. You can take 200 marks with you (about $200 in buying power at that time). In Paris there is a very small apartment, which friends of the Party have prepaid for six months and I have a contract with a small Austrian paper to write a weekly "Paris Reports" column."

So the three of us left the same day. Marriage in Berlin, border crossing by train. In Paris we took a taxi—our single and final luxury—to our apartment. It was a one-room place with a little gas stove, a sink and a bathroom. Life in exile began. As time went on, things got worse. Within six months, we had basically run out of money. We had made friends with some German and Austrian exiles, but they, too, were desperate. No one could obtain a work permit. So whatever money could be earned was "under the table"—just pennies.

I was fortunate to find a family who needed someone to clean house once a week. By mid-1936, the Austrian newspaper closed and that was the end of Goetz's income. He now had to rely on occasional work as a handyman and on a very small stipend from a German exile paper in Paris for which he wrote a weekly short story or a poem or two. A few times we got a little help from the Communist Party but that stopped when the refugees from Spain began to arrive in Paris.

The only thing that improved was our personal relationship. Almost immediately after our dramatic meeting, I felt myself attracted to this stranger with whom I now shared my life but he gave no sign of how he felt. We must have been in Paris for about a month when the first check from the Austrian paper came.

"Let's celebrate," Goetz suggested. "I'll get a bottle of wine."

During dinner he leaned toward me and that was our first kiss. We realized we were both in love and towards evening Goetz said: "Lucy, would you consider..." I interrupted him: "Goetz, you're too late, I recently got married and I'm completely devoted and faithful to my husband."

The evening turned into a celebration beyond expectations. As our love grew, it kept us going during these very difficult times. But soon another huge decision had to be made. There was a Jewish relief agency in Paris that we had contacted to see if there was any means to earn a living. Now they wrote us that there was a job open for which I was perfectly qualified: a nanny with a Jewish family in Johannesburg in South Africa.

Visas and tickets would be arranged by the employer. Marianne, of course, could come along. Free room and board, and $300 monthly salary. It was a very difficult decision and after days of thought and tears, we both decided I should accept for the sake of Marianne. Of course, I would try to get a job, passage and visa for Goetz as soon as possible. So, in December 1936 I began my second exile—this time in South Africa.

Now Goetz continued the story. "Life alone," he admitted, "was no fun. Paris is a wonderful city but if you have no money, it's like the tortures of Tantalus. All the pleasures possible are at your fingertips but when you reach for them, they elude you. It was, of course, a relief that I did not have to worry about feeding Lucy and Marianne, but I missed them both so much that in my depression I almost could not write any more. Dreary days and weeks. Christmas and New Year's were approaching. A friend from the Austrian exile community invited me for a holiday party at the Austrian Embassy. I declined. In my mood, nothing would be worth the effort and besides I had no decent clothes to wear to an Embassy event. My friend insisted and finally I agreed to go.

The food alone, I must admit, was worth it. Most of the afternoon—it was a cocktail party—I stood alone, very self-conscious in my old clothes. A gentleman approached me. He seemed familiar but I had no idea who he was or why I might know him. "I'm William Dieterle," he said. "I hear you're a writer. For an Austrian, that must be quite a problem, here in Paris. Are you fluent in French?"

"Oh no," I replied. "That is, 'no' to fluent, but 'yes' to 'it's a problem alright.'"

"Now after hearing his voice, I remembered who he was: a German actor / director who had left for Hollywood in the 30s. We began to talk. Evidently Dieterle had read some of my short stories, which he said he liked. Soon his wife Charlotte joined us. They asked if I was married and I briefly told them the strange story of Lucy. They seemed mildly interested. This was really not quite the small talk appropriate for an ambassadorial cocktail party and I began to feel extremely uncomfortable.

There was an awkward silence, then Charlotte said: "Listen, Mr. Mayer, we have to go to a formal dinner tonight so we must leave now and tomorrow we are on the way back to the U.S. But we would like to stay in touch. So here is our address, please give us yours. With that they left. My friend came over "Hey, not bad. That was Mr. Dieterle. He's very successful in Hollywood. Directing films for MGM."

Well, that was that. Of course, I never heard from them again, but I wrote Lucy and told her the story. I continued my meager existence. I found a young fellow who needed to learn German and I landed a job teaching him. One evening, as I came home, I found a note from the Credit Lyonnais. The bank said that there was a money order for $600 awaiting me. Obviously, there had been a mistake. Six hundred dollars was enough to live on comfortably for a month. I decided to ignore it but a few days later a second letter came. Best to set things straight. I was worried there might be an immigration problem, so I went to the bank with my Austrian passport firmly intending to prove that I was in Paris as a visitor.

At the bank I was directed to the Manager's office. "If you are, indeed, Mr. G. Mayer," he said, "we have a check for you for $600 from a Mr. Dieterle in Hollywood." What a shock! A few days later, a letter came from the Dieterles. They were back in Los Angeles, hoped all was well with me and asked me to confirm the arrival of the money. This was the beginning of an on-going correspondence.

Eventually, they suggested that I should come to the U.S. "There are many opportunities here," they said, "and if I wished, they would apply for an immigration visa for me and my family."

Of course I was enthusiastic. From then on, for three years a check for $600 arrived monthly. The Dieterles applied for a special visa. It had come this past November. They even booked our passage on the ZamZam. All I needed to do was to get to Cape Town. I was lucky to find a Portuguese freighter to take me.

As I listened to the story of the Mayers, the ZamZam was slowly steaming towards Brazil, across the South Atlantic. This was deemed the most dangerous part of the long voyage and the captain had suggested that all passengers wear life jackets at all times. Few did, but everyone was now on the lookout for any signs of a possible submarine. Meals were served during daylight only.

The danger was palpable but no one panicked when a U-boat alert was sounded by the captain. It was about 10 a.m. Someone had sighted a ship, or maybe a turret in the distance. Everyone scrambled for their life jackets and strained their eyes. Was it flotsam out there, an enemy ship, a friendly freighter? Something seemed to be there, but no one could agree on what it was.

Eventually, when nothing happened, tensions relaxed and the daily routine continued. At night, in total blackout, crew and passengers stayed on deck. We were blessed with very good weather and slept outdoors on balmy nights. I had lost my desire to associate with Les Bleus and spent most of my time with Goetz and Lucy.

After Cape Town, nightly dancing was moved to the afternoon and the band played on deck. Claire Marie was still somewhat in the picture. She came out for a drink or an hour of dancing when not on duty. We flirted lightheartedly, happy to be alive.

Impending danger gave spice to the adventure and romance.

As Goetz told his story, we marveled time and again at the amazing generosity of the Dieterles. Of course, we also talked about our plans for the future. My immediate destiny was pretty clear. My uncle had emigrated in 1938 to the U.S. He had now settled in Los Angeles and expected me to move there. The Mayers also assumed that they would go to Los Angeles where the Dieterles lived. So we made plans to travel together by bus from New York, across the United States, and to see the wondrous marvels of this immense country.

Lucy spent most of her time with Marianne, now almost six years old. With her quiet, soft-spoken voice, she played with her daughter, told her children's tales and listened happily to Marianne's chatter. I saw in Lucy an older sister and felt very comfortable around her. She was reading a book about evaluating the Rorschach Test.

Psychology was relatively new to me. My family, especially my uncle, had frowned on the idea of discussing one's problems with strangers. They considered it a sign of weakness. Thus, that science was rarely mentioned at home and, if so, only with disdain. I now found it very interesting and wanted to hear more—especially about a test, which could somehow measure and interpret character and personality.

I asked Lucy to give me the test but she refused. I kept bugging her and she kept refusing. I could not quite understand why she would not let me take the damn Rorschach. Many years later, it dawned on me that this kind of test is no game and one just does not fool around with it.

It took about 10 days to cross the South Atlantic. Then we moved along the east coast of Brazil and stopped at Recife. The evening before we docked, we all took part in an exuberant "Good Bye". The band and most French passengers were now leaving the ZamZam. Hotter and more humid than Mombasa, Recife was a typical equatorial port. We had arrived in the morning and were permitted to go on land. The ship was scheduled to leave that evening. Everyone was to be back on board by 7 p.m. The Mayers and I decided to take a taxi for a drive into "the jungle". In Portuguese-speaking Brazil, our German and French was useless. The locals spoke some dialect, probably not even Portuguese, so communication with the taxi driver was restricted to gestures.

It took a long time to convince him that we had no destination in mind, that we wanted him simply to drive us somewhere, anywhere into the countryside. The idea didn't make sense to him and for, at least, ten minutes, he refused to move. Finally, he seemed to understand and then we had to make sure that he understood that we needed to be back in time for the ship's departure.

We pointed to the ZamZam, then to our watches, which we made pointing to 6 o'clock. He nodded enthusiastically and off we went. We drove slowly. Alas! There was no jungle, just some agriculture and mostly open uncultivated land. The much-anticipated lions and elephants sadly were nowhere to be found.

We passed a number of small villages and eventually stopped at one of them. Its tavern was the destination our driver had decided was the perfect spot for lunch. Some excellent beer, along with all sorts of unknown food was served—none ordered by us since there was no menu presented. We ate and drank for well over an hour—excellent food as I remember and a very reasonable tab.

We then moved on, through more villages, all extremely poor, with unpaved roads and houses all made of clay. By 5 o'clock, we thought it was time to turn back. We tried to convey this to our driver who nodded approval and merrily continued on his way. As time went on, we became more and more worried. Clearly, we were hours away from the harbor, it was almost 6 o'clock and the ZamZam would certainly not wait for us.

The idea of being stranded in Recife was frightening. We screamed at the driver. We yelled. We showed him the watch and made noises like a ship's whistle—all to no avail. Our man was not to be disturbed. Eventually, we gave up. Marianne, who was with us, began to cry, aware of the distress of the grown-ups. We now drove in resigned silence, then the taxi turned off the main road, lumbered along an unpaved path, made some more turns and wound up a few hundred yards from the harbor. It stopped in front of the ZamZam at 10 minutes past six. Immensely relieved, we gave the driver what we hoped was a very big tip. I'm quite sure that had we not arrived in time, the ship would have sailed without us.

The next stop was Trinidad. By the end of December 1940, the Roosevelt Administration had passed a bill "Destroyers for Bases". It was one of many ways FDR helped England and later France, the USSR and China in their fight against the Nazis without directly getting involved in the European conflict. Under the provisions of this Act, the U.S. gave some of their destroyers to England in return for establishing U.S. naval bases in the Caribbean, including Trinidad.

Whatever the U.S. was doing in Trinidad was considered a military secret and, thus, no one was allowed ashore. We stayed only a day to take on fuel and food, then continued on past Cape Hatteras to New York—the final destination for most of us. The ZamZam would continue on to Boston, then return to Egypt. Claire Marie was to stay with the ship. The night before, we said our good-byes over a bottle of wine.

The ZamZam returned to Egypt via the same route. It left Boston with a number of American missionaries on the way to Africa. Half way across the South Atlantic, apparently in the area where we had had the submarine alert, the ship was stopped and sunk by a German submarine.

By luck, a German warship was in the vicinity and all passengers and crew were rescued and eventually interned in Germany. Since the U.S. was not yet at war, the capture of U.S. citizens became an international scandal. I heard of the sinking when someone told me that Life magazine had featured the story. Of course, I was relieved to know that Claire Marie was rescued; but as a French citizen now in German hands, her fate was very doubtful. I never heard from her, or of her, ever again.

We arrived in New York City on the morning of April 10th, three and a half months after leaving Port Said. An early breakfast was served and we were advised to pack and get ready for debarkation. Entering New York harbor, we passed the Statue of Liberty with its torch glistening in the sunlight. It was an emotional and exciting moment.

As we reached our assigned berth, we all were looking down from the deck to see if we could recognize any familiar faces. I had been told that a cousin of my mother, who had emigrated to New York two years earlier, would be waiting for me. He had been advised of my arrival and I was supposed to stay with his family in New York for a few days until I could arrange for the trip to Los Angeles. Since I had no idea what he looked like, I stopped looking down at the pier and, thus, was one of the first in line in front of the purser's office, for clearance to debark. As I faced the friendly and familiar ship's purser, he presented me with a bill for well over 800 dollars (2005 value).

"What's that?" I asked, stunned. "Well, these are the bar charges and other chits you signed. They have to be paid before you can leave the ship."

"But I don't have the money, I have less than $100."

"Well," he suggested, "you'd better let someone know you need a lot more. Is anyone waiting for you here?"

"Yes, a Mr. Held. But I don't know him and I'm not even sure he's here."

"In that case," my purser said, "you better sit down and wait. When all the passengers who are leaving now are cleared, we'll look for your Mr. Held."

By early afternoon I was called to the office. Someone was looking for me. Up the gangplank walked a vaguely familiar man, obviously my Uncle George. He had been standing at the dock, watching passengers as they departed but had found no Walter. Now that no one else seemed to be leaving the ship, he decided to look for me on board. Obviously happy to have found me, he greeted me most cordially but all that changed when he learned that I was in effect a prisoner of the ZamZam. Of course, he did not have $800 on him and, in effect, he would not be able to get it until the next day.

The purser was very understanding. "Not to worry," he told me, "you've been on board for nearly four months: an extra day here won't hurt you."

Uncle George left, only to return the following day with enough money to bail me out.

And so it was that I arrived in the New World, deeply in debt. My introduction to the institution of credit—so pleasant that first day at the bar of the ZamZam—had now ended in a painful crash.

The Helds—a family of four—had two daughters about my age. They lived in the Bronx in a very modest apartment. They, like most refugees, had lost their wealth when they left Germany. Now they made room for me by moving the girls into the parent's bedroom. Since they expected me to stay for only a few days, this was not a serious inconvenience.

I called Goetz the next morning to plan the trip to California. He did not know just exactly when they would leave. They were waiting for word from the Dieterles. Goetz felt he could not just arrive in Los Angeles and announce: "Here we are! Now help us again!" He was waiting for them to suggest the next step. Of course, he had notified them where he would be staying in New York, and he was sure he would hear from them shortly.

Great! That would give me a few days to see New York. My ignorance of all things American was incalculable. I fantasized that everything in this capital of America(!) would be different from anything I had ever seen. To some extent, that was true. Never had I seen so many cars. Never had I seen a building taller than six stories. But there were also disappointments. To me, New York meant skyscrapers; now I discovered that not every building really was a skyscraper.

The first two days, George took great pleasure to show me around Manhattan. He introduced me to the "Automat"—a restaurant where you could chose the food you wanted—all displayed in a row of little windows, which opened when you put money into the appropriate slot. No waiters: one carried one's own food to the table. And what a huge choice of wonderful delicacies were available to be tried! Now THAT was America!

He showed me Times Square and Rockefeller Center. We went to a movie in one of the great movie palaces where a vaudeville show preceded the film. And we went to an exhibition and saw a new technical wonder called television. It was wonderful and exciting but what I really wanted to do was to go to the top of a skyscraper to take in the view.

I had never been in a building higher than five-stories, so the thought of climbing up to the top of a 50- or 70-floor building and looking down was a great anticipated adventure. I thought this wish might be considered quite childish so I said nothing, but I vowed that soon I would find a way to fulfill my wish. I couldn't wait. On the third day, I was off to Manhattan alone. Full of anticipation, I went looking for an appropriate skyscraper. I strolled along Broadway and found an enormous office building. In the busy lobby were many elevators. I entered one together with six or seven other people.

In those days all elevators had a professional operator. He asked each of us for the floor. I replied: "73rd". The operator asked again and I repeated "Seventy-THIRD". My halting English was heavily accented and I had great trouble pronouncing "th". The operator still did not understand me and asked once more. I was so embarrassed that I just mumbled some excuse and left before he could close the door. OK, I had learned my lesson. Avoid "th" at all costs.

In the next building I asked for the 84th floor. "Whom do you want to see?" inquired the operator. That was so unexpected that I stammered: "Mr. Bodlander." He looked at the list of tenants: "There's no one in this building by that name. What address are you looking for? Since I had no idea, I left again, in shame.

I fared no better on the following try. When I asked for the 86th floor, I was informed that the building had only 82 floors.

Totally flustered, I decided to find buildings, which had no elevator operators. I found one and went up to the 57th floor. The doors opened directly to a receptionist's desk. "Whom did you come to see?" she asked sweetly. "Oh, obviously I'm on the wrong floor," I stammered, red-faced and retreated to the descending elevator.

Finally, finally, I ended up high in the hallway of a building on one of the top floors. There were no windows but there was a door at the end of the hallway, which opened to an indoor staircase. Light came from an enormous opening in the wall from a window with no glass panes in it, and for the first time in my life, I could look down on the world. The wall was wide enough for me to sit on the ledge of the window. I could see the tiny cars passing but I was so high up that no noise from the street reached me.

I sat knees up on the ledge for a long time, truly in heaven. Satisfied after a long, almost spiritual experience, it was time to go back down. I opened the door to the hallway. It was locked. Banging on the door had no effect. So I realized I would have to walk down. At each floor, I banged on the door, no one answered. After about 10 floors, the staircase led into the interior of the building and it became pitch dark—no windows, no lights.

Now I began to panic. On what floor was I? What would happen if I went past the main floor into the basement? Soon it was so dark that I could not even find the doors to the hallways. Lost and quite frightened, I climbed up again until I reached daylight and a window to the street. Yelling was useless. I thought I might draw attention by throwing some clothing down but then I realized that the wind would carry anything away quite distant from my "prison." Then I really became scared. No one knew where I was. No one could come to rescue me. After awhile, I calmed down.

The only thing to do was to go down again and to knock on the door of every floor. Six or seven stories down, still in daylight, a door opened. An astonished guard asked me what the hell I was doing there. Where did I come from? As I tried to explain, he told me how lucky I was. The building, like many others in Manhattan, was half empty. The top 30 floors were closed. He had been up on the 79th floor, quite by accident, to check on some electrical problem when he heard my knocking.

"If I had not found you, you might have died in that staircase," he said.

To this day, I think he was right. I went home that day, too embarrassed to tell anyone about my adventure. Much later I heard that the Empire State Building had an observation deck open to the public. Evidently, many other people shared my same desire.

called Goetz daily and every time the answer was the same: no word from the Dieterles. "Why don't you call them," I suggested. "That would be much too pushy," he felt. "After all they've done for me, I just can't impose on them. If they want me to come to California, they'll call. I'll just have to wait."

By now over a week had passed. A very angry phone call came from Los Angeles. My uncle—who, of course, had paid my ZamZam debt—wanted to know what was going on. I tried to explain, but was cut short. "Come to Los Angeles immediately. You're putting the Helds in an impossible situation. They are crammed and cannot put you up forever. A Greyhound ticket is waiting for you. Get on the bus today!"

The fury of a rich uncle was convincing. I left my friends in New York and began the Los Angeles trip alone. It took four days. We drove day and night and I did not see much of the country. Most impressive, however, was the desert across New Mexico, Arizona, and finally California. I had never seen landscapes like that. The Joshua trees, the bare treeless mountains, the exotic vegetation—all this was new and fascinating. I was happy to notice that these exciting sights were close to Los Angeles and promised myself that some day I would go back to visit.

I had always adored my uncle and now expected to be guided by him and be treated somewhat like a friend. I had no special plans and was ready for his suggestions. Most of all, I was happily anticipating to be with a close member of my family. It was not to be. My uncle greeted me coolly. He took me to a room that he had rented from a Mr. Shapiro, a door-to-door Fuller brush salesman, who was interested only in survival, and certainly not in me.

"Come to my apartment on Sunday, we'll go out for brunch," my uncle said and left.

With that, I was left to my own devices.

It was a bitter disappointment. I simply had not expected to be met with such obvious disinterest and for the first time in my life, I felt totally alone and lost. Life up until then had seemed so full of excitement and wonder. Every day had been a new adventure and every adventure a new challenge. Suddenly now, the joy was gone. I saw no future because I had no future.

Today, in retrospect, I can understand why my uncle was annoyed with me. He had paid for my class in the Haifa Teknion and I had refused to go along. In the U.S., I arrived in debt, which he made good. Then I had stayed in New York longer than he felt was appropriate. As a lifelong bachelor, he had next to no experience with young people and probably could not even imagine my needs and feelings. Well, he might have tried a little harder.

In 1941 the world was still in the throes of the Depression and Los Angeles was no exception. I knew I needed a job, but what was I trained for? In Germany, I had studied Latin and Greek; in Neuchatel, Economics and Literature; in Palestine, I had been a waiter. Now with barely any English, getting a job seemed impossible.

On my third day, I read in the newspaper of a job at a restaurant called The Chili Bowl. The Bowls were one of the first franchises in Los Angeles. They were cheap coffee shops housed in small round structures, symbolizing a chili bowl. They served coffee, sandwiches and, of course, chili. I called and was hired on the spot.

My job, in the outskirts of Los Angeles, started at 4 p.m. By bus it took almost an hour to get there, I was given a scrub brush and assigned to a sink full of greasy, dirty, tepid water. Huge pots crusted with grimy chili were to be washed in this stinking water and then rinsed. The water was not to be changed until the boss said so and that was never. The shift ended at midnight when the joint closed. Tired and disgusted, I asked for my money only to be told: "we pay every three days."

As everyone had already left, I asked the boss for directions to the bus. To his delight, I was informed that the busses stopped running at 11 o'clock. So I had to walk the night streets of Los Angeles, a lonely pedestrian, quite lost. I finally arrived home at four in the morning. I never went back to that hellhole and I never got paid. But all was not lost. In my mythology all U.S. immigrants who ended up as millionaires had started their careers as boot blacks. I started as a dish washer, so there as hope.

My next job was as shipping clerk at Cooper and Kramer—a men's clothing wholesale house on the 8th floor of the Cooper Building at Ninth and Los Angeles Street at the edge of downtown. The whole floor was filled with racks and racks of men's clothing—mostly dark suits and tuxedos. Underneath these racks were old open cigar boxes full of mothballs. My job was to collect these boxes, clean out the accumulated dust and lint, refill them with more mothballs as necessary and place them back again under the racks.

Occasionally, I was allowed to help the real shipping clerk with tasks like opening incoming merchandise or sealing outgoing parcels. The job paid $35 per week for the then standard eight-hour, six-day-workweek. It was sufficient to pay for my room and food, but not enough to have a life. Every day Mr. Cooper and Mr. Kramer went for lunch at the Pig-n-Whistle, an upscale watering hole near-by. Oh, how I envied them the luxury to visit such a fine restaurant! But on $32 a week that was beyond me.

Sunday brunches with my uncle became a tradition. I would walk to his apartment. Then we would take his car to a coffee shop on Wilshire and Western—always the same place. After-wards, we would take a stroll along the beautiful boulevard and end up at his place for a game of chess. One day, as we were walking, he asked me if I noticed a strange odor or was it his imagination. I, too, had noticed it. It was hard to define but it was definitely there. A week later we read in the Times that Los Angeles was experiencing an occasional day of bad air. It seemed a mixture of fog and smoke was hanging over the city. They called it "smog".

My social life was empty. I knew no one, was introduced to no one. Each day was the same as the next: streetcar to work, streetcar home. Would I ever meet anyone?

Work at Cooper and Kramer was unbearably boring. Mr. Cooper had a daughter who came to visit her father occasionally. Her name was Susan. About 18 or 19 years old, she had the looks of a movie star and she knew it. Her beauty was surpassed only by her arrogance.

One day I was at work, sitting on the floor, cleaning dusty mothball boxes, when Susan stopped by.

"So, you're Walter?"

"Yes."

"Well, I noticed you last time when I was here. This must be very boring work for you. Personally, I hate this place."

"Oh, it's a job," I replied.

"Dad tells me you're from Germany. What's it like there?"

Obviously, she wanted to talk, so I got up from under the clothes rack. Standing next to her, she was even more beautiful than I had imagined.

"What do you want to know?"

"Everything," she laughed and cocked her head slightly to the left. Our eyes met and it felt like an embrace.

"That would take a very long time," I told her.

"Look, I'm really interested." She was still smiling but her voice had become less playful. "Are you busy tonight? No? Good, then let's meet after work. I'll be in the lobby at 6."

Without waiting for an answer, she left, turned to throw me a most wonderfully flirtatious and warm smile. That evening we went across the street to the Pig n Whistle for cocktails. Susan took my arm. "Don't worry about paying. My dad has a tab here.

And for dinner we can go to Perino's. They know my family there and I can just sign the check."

Susan talked a lot but she also listened well and there was not a moment of awkward silence. We drove to Perino's in her convertible. At dinner I talked about Neuchatel and the Alps. She told me about her life and her desire for adventure. She invited me to their cabin in the mountains for the following weekend.

"Just you and me," she smiled. "The family is taking the yacht to Catalina."

This was really exciting and I wondered what Mr. Cooper would say when he heard about us. Of course, he would be shocked. But I knew Susan was deeply in love with me, so how could her father deny his daughter her greatest wish? At that moment the waiter in this most elegant restaurant brushed against our table and dropped a wine glass he was about to fill. The crunch made me look up. Mr. Cooper had just stepped into a mothball box and nearly fallen.

"Walter," he scolded, "these boxes are supposed to be under the racks, not in the aisles. So I resumed my dreary destiny. Tomorrow was time for another daydream.

Driven by loneliness and nostalgia for Neuchatel, Jeanette, Cyril and Pierre, I decided one day to go to the public library where I understood they had a foreign literature section. I wanted to re-read a book, which had been extremely popular in 1938.

It was called *Mon Petit* and was a very romantic story about a young Hungarian student who falls desperately in love with a French girl while studying in Paris. The very tender love story ends when the girl dies in an accident and the young man is left in desperate loneliness.

As I approached the area in the library where the book should be, there was a person standing in front of me. I waited awhile, finally said "excuse me" and brushed past him. At that moment he turned, and to our mutual astonishment, we recognized each other as acquaintances from Neuchatel. It was Henry Bamberger, a fellow classmate. What a fabulous coincidence. I was extremely happy suddenly to have found a person with whom I could talk about Jeanette, Pierre and Cyril—all of whom he knew. With this wonderful accidental meeting, my life suddenly seemed more bearable. Alas, it did not last long. Henry and I were very different people and though we stayed in touch, we never became friends.

15

My social isolation came to an end in early June when I heard of a liberal, social group called the APM—American Peace Movement. It was a political left-wing organization and here in Hollywood, it was made up of a number of young people who met weekly at various homes to discuss U.S. and world affairs. They accepted me with friendly interest and I was glad to have found people with whom I could share my views and feelings. Soon I felt part of the group.

Politically, their aims were completely in accord with my sympathies. We were working for Equality for Negroes (that was the then-accepted term), improved conditions for the "working man"—specifically, a 40-hour week for all, a minimum wage of 75 cents (it was then about 40 cents), and for more labor unions.

We disagreed when it came to international issues—at least for a little while. I wanted the U.S. to enter the war against the Nazis. My friends professed to be Pacifists and though they were emphatically anti-fascist, they did not want us to go to war. We had many friendly arguments and discussions about this.

Since Germany and the USSR were at peace, they saw the war as an imperialist adventure in which the U.S. should have no interest. It all changed when Germany invaded the USSR at the end of June 1941. The 'P' in APM changed from "Peace" to "People's" and the APM was now in the forefront, fighting for U.S. assistance to England and USSR. I was aware that our group was very much in-line with the Communist Party of the U.S., but that didn't bother me at all. For years, in Europe, the Communist parties were the most effective anti-fascists so they were my friends.

The news from Europe was terrible. By now Hitler had control of the entire continent and only England—weak and anemic after Dunkirk—stood in his way of complete victory. Though the constant bombing of English cities had not brought the war to an end, it seemed just a matter of time before Germany would defeat their last enemy and win the war.

Then on June 21, 1941, Hitler invaded the Soviet Union. I rejoiced at the news. This I believed would result in a complete turn around and eventually lead to the destruction of the Nazis. I was convinced that the Red Army would stand and fight and win.

Here in the U.S., I was, of course, in the minority. Daily, the newspapers and radio stations reported enormous German advances and the capture of huge numbers of Russian prisoners. Town after town was falling to the enemy. Commentators and political analysts speculated how long the Soviet army would be able to resist. Conventional wisdom gave them three weeks.

More sanguine experts expected a full Soviet defeat within 10 days. Optimists hoped for a month or two of resistance. My friends of the APM and I, hoped that Stalin had gained enough time during the Non-Aggression Pact to rebuild the Red Army and that the Soviet people would defend their country successfully. To the great relief of many and to the surprise of others, Churchill declared that England would do everything possible to help the USSR in their effort to defeat Germany.

American public opinion regarding foreign policy was fiercely divided. Many people had adopted an isolationist point of view after the U.S. involvement in WWI, and they were still convinced, in 1941, that the country should not be concerned in the affairs of Europe. Their slogan was "America First". They were mostly right-wing Republicans and their non-interventionist attitude favored, of course, the stronger power—Germany. The Roosevelt adminis-tration recognized the Nazi danger, wanted to help England and now the Soviet Union as much as possible, but was severely restricted by the fact that Congress—particularly the House— insisted on strict adherence of the Neutrality Act. Delicately Roosevelt managed to steer American policy toward assistance to the Allies through such measures as the "Cash and Carry" and "Lend Lease" Acts.

Hanging around with my friends from the APM, I began to learn English and to expand my vocabulary. On some Sundays, our group would go hiking in Griffith Park, and once, as we passed one of the numerous stables, someone suggested a horseback ride the following week. I was invited to join. One of the guys would pick me up on Sunday in his car, but I would have to return home by streetcar. Enthusiastically, I agreed.

"Did I know how to ride?"

Since my uncle rode in Germany, which I had thought that was the coolest thing, I, too, had wanted to ride (but never learned). So now I answered quickly with a convincing: "Yes, of course."

The following week at the stable I had to choose between a Western or an English saddle. I had no idea what they were talking about, but English sounded more sophisticated, so English it was.

It was very difficult to hide my clumsiness. No matter what I did, my horse decided not to budge. Everybody else was already moving along the trail, nearly out of sight. Finally, my old mare decided that it was time to go, so we followed the group. We rode for about half an hour, mostly at a leisurely gait—occasionally, at a trot. My English saddle was not a good choice.

From the moment I mounted the horse, I started to hurt. When it started a trot, it was torture. When we turned around, my horse woke up. Realizing that we were returning, it broke into an uncontrollable gallop and passed everybody. We were the first to arrive back at the stables. I dismounted and could barely walk. My friends took me to the streetcar and in my room I stripped. My behind was raw and bleeding. Resolved: I would learn how to ride.

The dreariness of each day was suffocating. How could I break out of this routine? I was trying to decide what to do with my life. Become a newsman? A teacher? I called the Board of

Education and arranged an interview with a gentleman who told me that I needed at least three more years of college.

"Besides," he told me, "there are no jobs open. In this Depression, schools have to save money. They are not hiring new teachers."

At Cooper and Kramer, every suit had a price tag on the sleeve. It was supposed to be a wholesale house, but most clients came in to buy just one or—at most—two suits. They were ushered through the aisles by one of the two owners and I could overhear the conversation. The buyer would look at the price tag and immediately complained that it was too expensive.

"What do you mean?" said Mr. Kramer. "At $45, this is a steal. It's pure wool, you know."

"Too much," said the customer.

"OK," conceded Mr. Kramer. "I'll let you have it for $30, but don't tell anyone."

They shook hands: the deal was done. I remember my shock when I realized that the price was totally an arbitrary number. There seemed to be some basic dishonesty in trade. Shouldn't the price be the same for everyone?

December came. It was quite warm. The climate was similar to that of Haifa. My English improved. I was now able to understand almost everything people said to me, but my accent—I was told—was still very strong. I had difficulty pronouncing "r's" and "th's".

Sunday breakfasts with my uncle became a pleasant routine. One day early in December I met him at his apartment and we drove to the usual Wilshire coffee shop. That Sunday the weather was absolutely beautiful and I hoped that after breakfast, my boring routine would be broken and that my uncle might invite me for a drive into the countryside. As we ordered our coffee, we heard a commotion in the street.

News vendors were shouting: "Extra, Extra, get your Extra!" We both wondered what might be happening. A new Russian defeat? That would hardly justify an extra edition of a newspaper. Had Russia capitulated? There was so much commotion in the street that I went and bought a paper. It was the news of Pearl

Skip to page 106 >

Harbor.   n the confessions as evidence of treachery. Today, I am sure that many of the accused were innocent, but among them were also those who were unquestionably dangerous pro-Nazis. I firmly believe the absence of a "Fifth Column" in the USSR was not accidental.

The United States had never seriously feared a foreign invasion. Now that Japan had attacked Pearl Harbor and declared war on the U.S., the possibility of a Japanese Fifth Column became a very real danger. California had a substantial Japanese population which during the previous century had not been treated fairly. They had been denied the right to U.S. citizenship, were not allowed to own land, and generally had been victims of racial discrimination.

The anger over Pearl Harbor, the fear of imminent invasion, and a very bad conscience led the general public to believe that the resident Japanese were an enormous threat and that most— or perhaps, many—of them were Fifth Columnists, planted by— and loyal to—the Tojo regime.

The order to arrest the Japanese and put them into camps far from the coast met with almost universal approval in California. I do not remember a single article in the papers against the measure. Personally, I, too, believed it was a very prudent and necessary act. Today, of course, I feel that the problem could have been handled differently and more fairly.

On our block in Hollywood, there was a small Japanese market and a nursery. They closed within a week after Pearl Harbor and disappeared. Thousands of Asians were displaced and interned without questioning; their properties confiscated.

Years later, a very small compensation was paid to these victims. At the time however, fear and rage were the controlling emotions and I cannot blame the Roosevelt administration for its decision. Decades later, when this breach of constitutional rights was acknowledged and tempers had calmed down, a more sincere apology and a much more generous compensation should have been forthcoming.

16

Once again the world was about to change—drastically, irrevocably, permanently. From that moment on, everyone was constantly listening to the radio. We heard Roosevelt's Day of Infamy address to Congress and we heard the Declaration of War against Japan. No word from or about Germany. Since I had been in the U.S. less than a year, I could not accurately gauge the national sentiment.

Here in Los Angeles, it was clear that people were angry, outraged and afraid. Within days, rumors had it that a large Japanese fleet was approaching California, that an invasion of Hawaii was imminent, that Japanese U-boats had been sighted off Los Angeles and San Francisco, that balloons loaded with gasoline were starting forest fires. None of these tales turned out to be true—except the last one. The Japanese did, indeed, try to start fires with incendiary balloons, which turned out to be completely ineffective.

Recent history had made the anti-fascist world aware of a very dangerous new strategic maneuver. Years before a military invasion, the Nazis had formed subversive pro-German cells in countries slated for attack. These cells consisted of Germans living in the foreign country and of natives whose sentiment was pro-Nazi. They would wait for the beginning of hostilities and then rise to sabotage the country's efforts to resist the invading

German forces. They were called the "Fifth Column" and they were extremely effective.

In Austria, Czechoslovakia, Norway, France, Romania, Yugoslavia and other countries before they were invaded, the Fifth Column had done its destructive work for the Nazis. By 1940 every country in danger of Fascist invasion feared that a Fifth Column might be lurking in their midst. The only exception was the Soviet Union. From 1936 on Stalin had started a systematic purge of the military.

The "Show Trials" in Moscow produced countless confessions from accused officers that, indeed, they had been anti-Soviet and /or German agents. Stalin's paranoia was not yet evident to the world at large and the Communist Parties of the Western nations had taken the confessions as evidence of treachery.

Today, I am sure that many of the accused were innocent, but among them were also those who were unquestionably dangerous pro-Nazis. I firmly believe the absence of a "Fifth Column" in the USSR was not accidental.

The United States had never seriously feared a foreign invasion. Now that Japan had attacked Pearl Harbor and declared war on the U.S., the possibility of a Japanese Fifth Column became a very real danger. California had a substantial Japanese population which during the previous century had not been treated fairly. They had been denied the right to U.S. citizenship, were not allowed to own land, and generally had been victims of racial discrimination.

The anger over Pearl Harbor, the fear of imminent invasion, and a very bad conscience led the general public to believe that the resident Japanese were an enormous threat and that most— or perhaps, many—of them were Fifth Columnists, planted by— and loyal to—the Tojo regime.

The order to arrest the Japanese and put them into camps far from the coast met with almost universal approval in California. I do not remember a single article in the papers against the measure. Personally, I, too, believed it was a very prudent and necessary act. Today, of course, I feel that the problem could have been handled differently and more fairly. On our block in Hollywood, there was a small Japanese market and a nursery. They closed within a week after Pearl Harbor and disappeared. Thousands of Asians were displaced and interned without questioning; their properties confiscated.

Years later, a very small compensation was paid to these victims. At the time however, fear and rage were the controlling emotions and I cannot blame the Roosevelt administration for its decision. Decades later, when this breach of constitutional rights was acknowledged and tempers had calmed down, a more sincere apology and a much more generous compensation should have been forthcoming.

few days after Pearl Harbor, Germany declared war on the U.S.—not the other way around, as it should have been! For me, these were heady days. I was now in a country at war with Germany. Maybe I could finally play a part in the war. The draft was now in full swing, young men were being called up for service on a daily basis. Sometime in late December, Congress passed a law that resident aliens could volunteer for service.

On January 5, 1942, I reported to the Armory in Los Angeles and by afternoon I found myself in Fort McArthur in San Pedro, inducted into the Army. About 400 of us were sworn in that day. Most were assigned to Infantry but those who had volunteered were allowed to choose the branch they wanted.

I chose Field Artillery. We were ordered to pack up our civilian clothes and were issued uniforms. Those woolen, olive shirts, trousers and jackets were called "ODs" (olive drab) and to my surprise, they fit well. Even the boots, available in all sizes were comfortable. The helmets were from WWI—flat and similar to the ones the Brits wore in all those romantic war movies of the 30s. Thus, a bunch of rather non-descript civilians were transformed into look-alike GIs (Government Issue).

The next morning, a truck convoy transported us to Camp Roberts, near Paso Robles, for Basic Training. Infantry and Field

Artillery were housed in different areas of the camp and our training was specific to the branch. Basic Training was to last nine weeks. It consisted mostly of what one would expect. Daily "fall-in" for roll call, followed by one hour of calisthenics, then depending on the day, 5 and 10-mile hikes, rifle instruction, practice on the rifle firing range, lessons of the do's and don'ts in the Army, introduction to the various guns of our Field Artillery and endless hours of waiting for nothing in particular.

The barracks had bunks for 40 men, and when there was no specific task to perform these barracks served not only as sleeping quarters but became poker and crap saloons. Thus I was introduced to gambling of which I knew absolutely nothing.

For my family when I was growing up in Breslau, cards were "beyond the Pale." I was not allowed to touch them. To this day I remember the frequent incantations of my uncle about the most dangerous vices tempting young boys. "Wine, women and cards. Stay away from wine, women and cards!" These were the admonitions given to the 10-year old and whether in jest or not, I took them quite seriously. For sure the family abhorred any form of gambling.

After WWII there was a very successful TV show called Sergeant Bilko. The hero was a conniving but kindly fellow, who supplemented his meager army pay by running all kinds of card and dice games. Bilko was a perfect reconstruction of the many pals I encountered in the army. I joined the games with wild abandon and accepted my bad luck as part of the learning process. It never occurred to me that I might be swindled by theses nice comrades.

We got paid every two weeks: one dollar a day, 30 dollars a month. Some money went for beer at the bars of Paso Robles, but most went to my gambling friends. Weekends were free and we were allowed to leave. Camp Roberts is about a three-hour drive from Los Angeles and in those days, hitchhiking was the normal way for soldiers to travel. Every one gave us a lift; there was never a problem. This wonderful public attitude lasted well beyond the war and began to change only in the late 50s when more and more crimes started to be reported. I caught a ride "home" regularly, proudly displaying my uniformed self to my uncle. Whether he was impressed or not, I don't know. After my second month in the army, he asked me how much money I had saved and when I admitted that the coffers were practically empty, he was not amused. Proudly, I can say I never asked him for money, and proudly, he never offered any.

A very different offer, however, did come my way. One day after roll call, our sergeant—a grizzly old professional soldier—asked who among us had gone to college. I did not know if my Swiss schooling counted as college but when I explained that I had been in schools for 14 years he decided I qualified. Qualified for what? Officers Training School!! I could not believe my ears.

They wanted me to apply for training to become an officer in the United States Army. Me, the reject from the French army; me, the shipping clerk from Cooper & Kramer; me, who had been in this wondrous country for less than a year! Me, an officer?!

One must remember I had grown up in Germany where any uniform meant power and authority, where an army uniform meant honor and respect and where an officer of the army was admired and obeyed by all. It seemed inconceivable that I could really be considered for such an honor. I filled out the necessary paperwork and for days could hardly sleep.

The excitement of this enormous possibility was all consuming. Of course, I said nothing to my uncle, nothing to the fellows around me. I was told I would have to wait for at least two weeks and, indeed, eventually, I was called before an examining board consisting of five officers. After a few rather inconsequential questions, I was dismissed.

Three days later came the verdict: Rejected. No reason. No explanation. My sergeant noticed my despair and took me aside. "It must be your strong accent," he said. "Try again in a few months." I said nothing but I was determined never to apply again, never to go through such exalted hopes and terrible humiliation again. Toward the end of the Basic Training period our battery (company) went on maneuvers to an artillery firing range at the nearby Hunter

Liggett Reservation. In long truck convoys we drove through central California towing our huge 155 mm howitzers to their destination in rugged mountain terrain. The exercise was to last a few days and we were expected to sleep on the ground with no tent and no sleeping bags. Each evening we sat shivering around campfires trying to fall asleep in the most ungodly cold I could ever remember. I had no idea that sub-tropical sunny California could be so miserable.

Finally the big day came. We had completed Basic Training and everyone was assigned to his permanent unit. Lists were posted: some men were going to divisions in Florida; others, to Montana, Oklahoma or elsewhere in the U.S. Everyone was excited, everyone was saying good bye to the short friendships they had formed and everyone was packing their duffle bags. Not me.

My name was on not on any list. I reported to the sergeant, he asked the lieutenant. No one knew what was going on, but it was certain that I was "unassigned". Next day the barracks at Camp Roberts grew quiet, I was alone until a new batch of recruits arrived and the Basic Training routine began again. Since I had just completed my stint, I did not have to submit to another 60 days of training, but no one knew what to do with me. I was again the lone outsider. Eventually, I heard that there was a group of us foreigners at Camp Roberts and that the Army had no idea what to do with us "enemy aliens".

Early in May, Congress came to our assistance. They passed a bill that aliens in the service could apply for immediate citizenship. There were some 20 other aliens at Camp Roberts. We were loaded into a truck and dispatched to the Superior Court in San Louis Obispo where we were sworn in as citizens of the U.S. in a five-minute ceremony and sent back to Camp Roberts.

One week later I was assigned to an artillery brigade stationed at Camp Forrest, Tennessee. I was given a train ticket to Lebanon, where a truck waited to bring me to my unit. As I reported for duty, the First Sergeant of the Battery asked if I knew how to drive. What a wonderful question. I answered of course:

"Yes," which, by the way, was not entirely true. I loved to drive but I lacked experience. Though I had had no car, in Haifa, I had enrolled in a driving school. In broken German, the instructor insisted that one had to understand the workings of an engine before one could drive a car. So for hours I had heard of clutches, gears, cylinders and other mechanical terms and most of it went right over my head.

When he finally let me start to drive, the instructor kept yelling: "Watch the road, not your foot, you idiot." But the idiot had to look down to find the clutch rather than the accelerator or the brake. Slowly and painfully, after several weeks, I finished the course and took the test. After failing twice, I got my license and that had been the extent of my driving experience.

"You can drive? Good," said the sergeant. "You will be assigned to that Diamond T and he pointed to the largest truck I had ever seen. It was what they called a Prime Mover, designed to tow a 155-mm gun, the largest cannon in the army's arsenal.

"Here's the key, try it out."

As I climbed into the driver's seat (which was higher than I was tall), I began to wonder about my white lie.

"Put it in first," the sergeant said, as he sat next to me.

Slowly the monster began to move. "You have to double clutch for each gear," the sergeant continued and as I tried to move into second gear, he yelled: "Double clutch, damn it! Double clutch!"

His angry screams, the grinding noise of the abused gears, my inability to shift into second... I was right back at the driving school in Haifa. But the sergeant was a kind soul.

"Stop the truck," he ordered and then he explained what "double clutch" meant and how to do it. As we moved on, I practiced shifting from gear to gear.

"Have you ever towed anything?" he asked next.

This time I decided to be truthful: "No, never."

"Well," he laughed, "we'll have some fun, the 155 are pretty big. You'd better get some experience before we go on maneuvers."

For the next few days, I towed the 155 backwards and forwards, into driveways, out of alleys, through fields and gullies. I jack-knifed the gun so many times that even my kind sergeant finally lost patience.

"From tomorrow on," he said, "you'll drive the lieutenant. I hope you'll do better with the jeep." Finally, I had found my calling. Driving a jeep was fun and easy.

Almost all the men in my Battery were from the South or the Mid-West, and most of them had been drafted directly out of the Civilian Conservation Corps (CCC). This was one of the New Deal ideas created to combat the terrible unemployment during the Depression. Young men, ages 18 to 24—most of them with little education and unable to find work—could enroll in the CCC. The Corps was run much like the army with its mission to build roads, maintain National Parks, fight forest fires and plant trees in areas devastated by the windstorms of the 30s.

The pay, just like the Army's was $1 a day. Strict discipline was imposed, but the work was healthy, three meals a day were guaranteed. Since everyone was there by choice, the morale was good. These rugged guys were my idea of the Old West cowboys, and I found them as interesting as they found me strange. To them, I was this city boy with a funny accent from far-away Europe. When they spoke of me they referred to me as the "Heini" which at that time identified a German.

To a man, they were kind to me but they teased me mercilessly and frequently without my even being aware of it. I still had trouble pronouncing "r", "th", and "w" properly. Once I was told to get some blankets. As I returned, someone asked where I had been. It was a perfectly innocent question but it soon became the question most often asked of me. I had answered: "the supply room." Deafening laughter from my pals. "Where? Tell us again."

"The supply room." It became a standard joke. They called strangers over to ask me where blankets are stored. "In the supply room!" I was always a success. I knew something was funny but I had no idea what and no one told me. Much later I realized that what they had heard me say was "the supply womb". Oh well…

In July 1942, my Division went on maneuvers. We packed our bags, mounted our vehicles and drove in long convoys through the mountainous wilderness of Tennessee. It was my first chance to see rural America and I expected jubilant patriotic crowds to greet us as we drove through the towns. Instead, we passed empty streets and shuttered stores. Not a person in sight. As I was driving the lieutenant's jeep, I finally asked him what was going on.

"I think," he said, "they are afraid of us. They probably believe the Yankees are coming back to reoccupy the South."

He was right. The rural South—just recently electrified—had no radio, no newspaper and generally had not heard that the country was at war. We had broken into their isolation. They were stunned and suspicious. But it did not take long for their attitude to change. The "Yankees" turned out to be boys from all over the U.S., and soon the merchants and bars of Tullahoma and Lebanon greeted us GIs with open arms and cash registers.

Field Artillery has something to do with elementary trigonometry. The four guns of a battery are supposed to be mounted in such away that all four guns point at a target parallel to each other. That is called to "lay the battery". You achieve this by using basic instruments similar to surveying tools and a little trig. Usually, this was the done by the Second Lieutenant but since I was his driver and we were on friendly terms, he allowed me to "lay the battery" on occasion. It was fun and challenging.

Maneuvers for us meant to drive to some designated wilderness area, lay the battery as fast as possible, and start firing at a distant target too far away to be seen from the gun emplacement. The Forward Observer, one of our officers hidden in a tree top or a church steeple of a nearby village close enough to "the front" to see the target, would communicate with us by field telephone to tell us whether we had overshot the target or were short of it. We would then correct the gun position and fire again. The idea was not only to hit the target, but to hit it as fast as possible. Time was of the essence. The targets were wooden tanks; the ammunition was live.

The maneuver was to last two weeks but toward the end of the second week, we were told the Division had flunked the test, was not yet "battle worthy" and would stay in the field for another month. I liked the outdoor life in the mountains of Tennessee. It was easy and fun.

The day began with a warm breakfast from the field kitchen, then a drive to some location where we were to lay the battery, and fire at the "enemy" until we hit the target. Then usually a five-mile hike—just to stay in shape—followed by more firing practice, Lunch from K-rations (small cardboard packages containing food bars, full of vitamins and some candy)—all rather tasty.

The afternoon was spent driving to a new encampment and digging new foxholes. The field kitchen was already waiting there with the hot dinner, then we were free for dice or card games until night fell. By then, I had learned my lesson and rarely got involved in gambling.

We were allowed to have campfires and so every evening after dark, my comrades built a fire. Several guitars appeared and the songs and ballads of the old West and the South wafted through the air. This was a magical time. The songs were new to me but seemed familiar. There were some army songs from WWI, there were the hillbilly and country songs and there were folk songs from the Depression, which was still ongoing.

As time went by, I learned some of these songs and joined in, at least, partially. Those nights were reminiscent of my Boy Scout years in Germany, and as a city boy I had found the outdoor life totally romantic. My fellow soldiers, so unsophisticated, were, in fact, far more sophisticated than this funny foreign "Heini" in their midst.

The gathering of wood for the fire, the songs, the stories told and listened to, the jokes told and retold, all this was daily fare to them. They had lived this for the last few years in the CCC camps, and to them, there was nothing romantic about all this. The fun in their life was this stranger from Europe who obviously did not have a clue. So the tall tales began and became taller every night. One guy told of his encounter with a bear in Oregon, then another would chime in: "You know, they have bears and wolves here in

Tennessee." Then still another would tell how he slept with the wife of his commander in the CCC but escaped in the last moment just before the husband arrived unexpectedly. Every night I would listen to these stories. They all ended in good-natured laughter— much of it because they realized that most of what was going on was way over my head.

Toward the beginning of the third week in the field, someone started talking about hunting. "We ought to have a little hunting party," one said.

"No," replied another. "Not enough rabbits around here."

"Well, I wasn't thinking of rabbits necessarily, don't they have plenty of deer around here?"

"Yeah," chimed in another. "Deer and foxes."

"Come on," another voice chimed in. "Tennessee is known for its snipes."

"Yeah," they all agreed. "There must be plenty of snipes around."

The banter went on, back and forth. I listened excitedly and tried to join in.

"You mean they would allow us to go hunting at night?"

"Sure, but not tonight, it's too late now."

Next night I started again: "Hey, let's go hunting. That would be fun." A few thought it was a good idea but most of them agreed that you couldn't hunt when the moon was out.

"Well," said one, "we could always catch some snipes. They're running now."

"Are you crazy?" Said another. "Snipes hide until the moon has disappeared."

"What are snipes?" I asked.

"Oh, they're little creatures. Really fun to hunt. Everyone had a snipe story to tell. They all sounded exciting.

"Come on, let's go tonight," I insisted.

"No," they all laughed. "But soon." So it went on like this for a few evenings and then, one night, a guy said he had permission to take the jeep out for a night of snipe hunting.

"Who wants to go?"

Six or seven stood up. I, too, wanted to go but I didn't seem to have a chance.

"We can't take more than four." So I was out. But one of my friends said: "Let the Heini go, it would be a new experience for him."

So I found myself in the jeep, ready for my first snipe-hunting adventure. We drove about 10 miles and came to a large field. In the far distance, one could barely see the outline of the woods. The night was pitch black. During the ride everyone was very excited. Then they stopped the jeep.

"Here, Walter, take this paper bag and a flashlight. Go about 100 yards into the field. Do you see the woods over there? OK, we'll drive there and then we'll start walking in your direction making an enormous amount of noise. That will arouse the snipes and they will start to run away from us, towards you. When they are close enough so you can hear them, open the bag, hold it close to the ground and turn on the flashlight. The snipes will be blinded by the light and run right into your bag. You'll probably not get more than two or three, but if you close the bag fast enough, they'll stay in there."

With that, they left me and as I started to walk into the field. They yelled the last instructions: "Don't turn on the flashlight until you hear the snipes. Good luck!"

As the sounds of the disappearing jeep faded away, I stumbled into a farmer's potato patch not sure how far I should go. In the distance, I could barely see the outline of the forest. As I stopped and opened my bag, my eyes became used to the darkness. I heard the engine of a car, but saw no light. Some bird cried out briefly, then there was total silence.

The stars were shining bright in the dark. After awhile, I wanted to sit down but the ground was too damp. By then my friends should have emerged from the woods. I stood up. I squatted. I waited. I heard an owl hoot. Then again: the silence of the night. On the distant horizon loomed the outline of the woods, but no noisy friends chasing snipes appeared. I was holding the bag wide open ready for the snipes and my fellow hunters. But there wasn't a sound.

It took a good hour for me to realize that I had been had, and it took the rest of the night to find my way back to the Unit. In the morning, they greeted me with great merriment. Many years later, after the war, some friends in Los Angeles suggested one evening that we should go grunion hunting. "Grunion are small fish," my friends told me, "and you go out late at night to the beach with a flashlight and just pick the grunions as they wash up on the sand."

Needless to say, I did not fall for that one. The next day, I read in the newspaper that the grunion were running. Accompanying the story were photos of a happy group of people scooping up the little fish. Oh well, another missed opportunity.

18

The maneuvers continued and so did the routine. The army hated idle soldiers and cleanliness came to the rescue. If there was nothing to do, we were ordered to put a new coat of paint on a jeep or a cannon or whatever. Anything could be painted with the all-pervasive OD (olive drab).

"Hurry up and wait" was the main motto of military life and "police the area" was the oft-heard order to keep us busy when there was nothing else to do. Among my favorites was: Alphabetize this, then burn it.

"Police" meant to spread out over an area, for example, a campsite, and to pick up everything that had not been there before we had arrived. This led to the expression: "If it's there, pick it up. If you can't pick it up, paint it. If you can't paint it, piss on it."

Thus the days dragged on and we were still on maneuvers. It was now the summer of '42. Then one morning I received orders to leave the maneuver area and to report to the medic at Camp Forrest. At the clinic, I told the doctor—a captain—that I was not on sick call. There must have been a mistake.

"Just strip to your shorts," he ordered and proceeded to give me as cursory a physical as I had ever had. After finding that my heart and lungs were exactly where they were supposed to be, he dismissed me with a friendly handshake and a jovial: "Well, you're in fine shape. Good luck." I was completely baffled. First of all, this was not how officers dealt with enlisted men. They did not shake hands and then what was the meaning of that "good luck"? For what?

When I asked the doc: "Oh, you don't know?" he smiled. The physical is the last step on your way to OCS. Your application was approved last week and tomorrow you are on the way to Officers Candidate School at Fort Sill.

It is hard to say whether I was more dazed, excited or bewildered as I went to pack my duffle bag. After the enormous elation and terrible disappointment following my previous application and subsequent rejection for OCS, I had meant it when I vowed never to apply again. Now, not only had I "applied" but I had been accepted—all without my knowledge. That evening the first sergeant came in from maneuvers to talk with me. Aware of my first attempt for OCS, he had decided with the consent of our battery commander to submit an application for me, forging my signature. He was pleased with my excitement and he, too, wished me the best of luck.

Today, I barely remember the man, certainly I can't recall his name. It is sad that people who so drastically influence our future often disappear into the dim fog of the past. This nameless sergeant made my days in the army much easier and may have saved my life. I'm grateful for his confidence in me and I thank him for that. Although I was re-assigned to the same division later, I never saw him again.

Fort Sill is close to Lawton, Oklahoma, and that was where the 12 men from my division, all ordered to OCS, were greeted by an unsmiling lieutenant.

"Take a good look at the town, as we drive through it," he said. "Look at the bars and the movie theater. It's the last time you'll see them. Once you're in Fort Sill, the only way to get out is to flunk out. For the next 90 days there's no leave, no weekend passes, just work. But don't worry, most of you won't make it anyway." With that cordial greeting began the three most amazing months of my life.

As we arrived in camp, we were escorted to a hall for an introductory briefing. About two hundred new cadets waited until a captain gave us the rules and conditions of OCS.

"You are class No. 50," he said. "You will be randomly divided into 6 batteries of 32 men each. Each battery will be housed in four tented huts, eight men per hut. You will receive the list of names of your 32 fellow Battery candidates and you are expected to know each other by name within eight hours.

"On Monday mornings each week, you will receive a printed schedule which will tell you where you are to report for the next seven days and at what time. Each Battery will select a "commanding non-com," who will be responsible to assemble and march you to the appropriate location. For the first 30 days, you will always march together and always stand at "attention" while waiting. You will never go anywhere by yourself. The second 30 days you will stand at "parade rest" while in formation. If you should make it to the last 30 days, you will be allowed to stand "at ease" and occasionally go alone to classes or the PX (Post Exchange, something like a drug store).

"All officers you pass are to be saluted and when spoken to, you will address them as 'Sir'. For every infraction of rules, you will receive a 'gig'. Twelve gigs in any one week and you're out. When you have 20 gigs, you will receive a written warning; 25 gigs, a final warning, the 26th gig, will return you back to your Unit.

You will receive one gig for a grade below 'C' in your classes, one each for badly shined shoes, for being late, for a wrinkle on your bed, for not being in uniform, for not standing at attention or parade rest, for not saluting an officer. You can also be flunked out by any officer at any time. For the first two months, you will go to the bathroom only at specified times and will not be excused at any other time."

Then he paused. After a short pause, he continued. "At the end of the fourth week, you will have to pass a major obstacle. You will be asked to grade your fellow Battery members on a scale from 1 to 5—5 being the best. You are to judge how good you think an officer each candidate might be. The 10 soldiers with the lowest score will be flunked."There was another pause, then: "Now remember, it costs a lot of money to train you monkeys, we all want you to succeed but we will be tough and experience tells us that many of you will not make it."

His tone suddenly changed and became almost mellow. "It's not a disgrace to flunk out. Should it happen to you, you will be promoted one rank and sent to a unit of your choice. Now, go to work and do your best. Attention! Dismissed."

I was very impressed, very scared and very determined to pass. I wrote my uncle that I was on extended maneuvers and would not be able to be in touch with him for a few months. I did not want him to know I was at OCS because I did not want to face his scorn should I fail.

The next three months for me were totally amazing. I surrendered completely to army discipline and became just a cog in the vast machinery that was OCS. There were classes to pass: Military History, Geometry, Trigonometry, Ballistics, Artillery in Theory and Tactics are among the ones I remember. There were 5- and 10-mile marches to complete, shoes to shine, bunks to be made, uniforms to press, officers to salute and obstacle courses to pass. We were constantly scrutinized.

The day started at 6 a.m. with 30 minutes of calisthenics, then a march to the mess hall for breakfast and it ended at 8 p.m. after a march from the Mess Hall to our tent. Everything was timed to the minute. Lights out at 10 p.m. The time after dinner was expected to be spent studying. The organization was flawless. Gone were the days of "Hurry up and wait."

Now every move was precise; every minute accounted for. I found this machine-like precision quite helpful. Here and later in combat, my German Boy Scout experience was extremely helpful. I had learned to submit unconditionally to total discipline and to physically push myself to the extreme. After the first two weeks we began Field Exercises. These were the most interesting and the most important parts of our training. Each day we were trucked to a "command post" somewhere in the wilderness. The training officer pointed out a target, maybe a house or a car or a simulated tank, barely visible, a few miles away. With a field telephone in one hand and binoculars in the other, we were to give orders to a Battery of four howitzers located somewhere behind us. Each candidate had five tries to hit the target. You would calculate the coordinates, order the Battery to fire and then look for the puff of smoke—the impact.

Short of the target, you would increase the range—too far to one side and you would have to change the coordinates. So you stood there, shouting "Fire" into the phone and looked... and nothing happened! No puff, no dust, nothing. You must have missed something, so you looked and looked and sweated and suddenly the instructing officer yelled: "Do something!" so you would give orders to increase the range and hope that this time, you would see the hit.

The trouble was that often there was a depression between you and the target and if the shells hit there, you could not see the impact. If you panicked and did nothing for too long, you were penalized with a gig. If you did not hit close to the target after five tries, another gig.

Every week I crossed off the names of fellow candidates who were "out" and by the beginning of the final month, just 19 of the original 32 were left. Now we could stand "at ease" and the discipline, in general, was less intense. Soon we were ordered to assemble for "measuring". It was our first excursion into nearby Lawton to a local shop where our new officers uniforms were tailored. Then came a trip to the hat shop for proper headgear and a few days later, the final fitting. It became clear that the end was in sight and we had made it.

Soon the night before graduation was on hand. We were allowed all the liquor we wanted, could move freely from tent to tent and we celebrated deep into the night. We were intoxicated with the realization that we had accomplished an enormous task. Next morning, dressed in our new officers uniform, we marched to the graduation ceremony. A band played, just for us, every trumpet every drum a musical congratulation. The camp commander's speech was mercifully short and ended just in time for breakfast. Fort Sill's OCS class No. 50 was dismissed: 94 of us had made it. We received our new assignments and a two-week leave.

Second Lieutenants were called "Shave-Tails". To this day I have no idea what that means, but I suppose it implies that we were young, inexperienced, and probably incompetent and this is exactly how we were treated by our superior officers.

But at the time, the glory of the wonderful new uniforms, the prestige of being an officer, the elixir of having passed 12 weeks of grueling tests gave us a bounce and a glow, which we thought would last forever. Tradition had it, we were told, that the first soldier to salute us should get a 1 dollar bill. Immediately upon graduation, we were saluted by a sea of "admiring" enlisted men and each one got his dollar—a day's pay at that time.

I took my two weeks leave in Los Angeles. At Fort Sill we were told that we could go to any airport and look for the ATC (Air Transport Command) offices. Every army plane was under control of the ATC and any officer had the right to hitch a seat on any plane. The only condition: You had to have a parachute. Most army air installations had parachutes; you could simply take one and then leave it at your destination for the next guy. Occasionally, when there were no parachutes available, one had to wait for a plane to come in and hopefully someone would get off and one could then get his parachute.

The system worked very well and whenever I had a leave, I used the ATC. Sometimes you would get a ride on a disabled bomber on the way to a repair station, sometimes you would have to fly far out of your way but somehow you could always manage get to the final destination.

Curiously, as happy as I was, I don't remember my uncle's reaction when he saw me in my new rank and uniform. It was an immense disappointment that he took so little notice of—what to me—was an important achievement. To be an officer in the U.S. Army, I felt, was something to be proud of and proud I was, but it was not to be shared with him. As a young boy and later into my teens, I had adored my uncle. In Germany, he had been the co-owner of one of Europe's largest import-export companies. Fresh and dried fruit—the export; canned goods and spices, the import. He had achieved his position of great wealth and power by working steadily and brilliantly in the same company in which he grew up, and he grew with it, being promoted, step by step, until the owner of the firm offered him a full partnership.

He lived in Breslau, as we did, but his life style was far more grandiose than ours. "Grandiose" may not be the right word since it implies pomp and ostentation, and my uncle certainly did not reflect these rather cheap qualities. To the contrary, he lived a very private, though very comfortable, life. Most of all, he had style, grace and education. Like many assimilated German Jews, he also had a well-developed sense of national pride. He admired and emulated what he considered Prussian values, such as obedience, tact, honor, and above all honesty and correctness.

My parents lived a very different life style. My father ran a small family business, a factory and wholesale enterprise, manufacturing paint pigments and house painters tools. Business was often shaky, subject to the harsh conditions of the inflation of 1925 and the depression of the 1930s. In our house, intellect was king. My father read lovingly the most esoteric philosophers—Kant, Nietzsche, Schopenhauer—and, of course, the classics—Goethe, Schiller and Lessing. Many Saturday afternoons I would sit on the arm of his overstuffed leather chair while he read and explained to me the poems and plays of the German writers. My father was a convinced atheist and though he insisted that I not be indoctrinated into any religion, he did, on those Sunday afternoons include reading and discussion of the Bible. I loved those hours together and regretted that they had to end when, at 15, I left to school in Neuchatel.

Sundays in Breslau were frequently spent at my uncle's spacious place where, after the noon meal, my father and uncle would play games of chess, which my father usually won. They both smoked cigars and I was allowed to watch and listen as they discussed economics and politics between games. Occasionally, as my parents returned home, I was allowed to "stay over".

Next morning at breakfast, I could ask all the questions I wanted about politics, philosophy or simple personal problems, and my uncle would answer and discuss these things with me. At that time I was between the ages of five and 13. And, he answered as seriously as if I were an adult. He knew I admired him and he, too, must have enjoyed these years. Later as I grew up with my own ideas and did not fulfill his expectations, he became disillusioned and eventually apparently disinterested.

The two weeks leave in Los Angeles went by slowly. I called a girl I had once met who reminded me of Jeanette. We had a few boring dates, clearly she liked my uniform but not the person who was wearing it. The disinterest was mutual. Eventually, quite disappointed, I left Los Angeles and reported to the same division— but to a different battery—in Tennessee. The division was still on maneuvers; they had again flunked the "efficiency test" and were still trying to achieve "combat ready" status.

My new assignment was Forward Observer. In the old days the FO had to find high ground or a building from which to observe the result of the firing and to communicate with the gun position how to correct their aim in order to hit the target. Now, in the modern era of WWII, the FO was assigned a plane and a pilot. Mine was an open two-seat Piper Cub, which could land and take off on a dime. Strangely, the pilots were not officers. They were sergeants (non-commissioned officers, who were paid much lower wages than commissioned officers) and understandably they were resentful since they were certainly as important to the mission as the "dumb" second lieutenant next to them.

When I was introduced to my pilot, he asked if I had ever flown before. I had not. "Well," he said, "let's take a little practice ride." We took off and flew about 3,000 feet over the Tennessee forests for a few moments. We tested the radio. He showed me the controls. It was a beautiful smooth ride and a great first experience for me.

Suddenly, the engine began to sputter, it stopped and we began a steep dive. Fortunately, the pilot got the engine started again and as we climbed he looked at me and smiled sickly: "that was a close call". We had just gained some altitude when the engine went out again. This time we were gliding lower and lower, the landing gear began to brush the treetops.

"We're out of gas!" the pilot shouted.

I was certain we would crash. We did not. As we approached the landing area, the plane suddenly regained power, we climbed, circled the base and landed smoothly. "Well, you behaved better than I expected from an officer," the sergeant smiled.

"Of course, you know, we had plenty of fuel all the time."

We became a good team but it didn't last very long. Every officer had a secondary assignment and mine was "Mess Officer" for the regiment, responsible for clean and sanitary kitchens. While on maneuvers, the job was to assure that enough warm food was served daily. A nothing job since the mess in each battery runs pretty much by itself.

Walter, 5, on his first day of school in Breslau, Germany, 1925.

Walter's mother with her brother, who organized their visas and voyage to the United States. Photo: mid-1930s.

Walter's parents, 1932
Breslau, Germany (now Poland)

Walter, 15, shortly before he left for Neuchatel.

Bei dem Geräte-Wetturnen
der Reichsjugendwettkämpfe
1934 in Breslau
veranstaltet unter der Förderung des
Oberbürgermeisters
errang den Sieg

Walter Bodlaender

Stadtamt für Jugendertüchtigung

Stadtrat

Stadtturnrat

Left: Certificate showing that Walter had won First Place in the Reich Youth Athletic Competition in his hometown Breslau in 1934.

Foreign youth who were boarders at the Webers in Neuchatel, 1935. Walter, in center (white shirt) behind Mr. Weber; Francois (far right).

Walter Bodlander, Young German Refugee, Now in Uncle Sam's Army

By TOM CULLEN *

LOS ANGELES, Jan. 26.— Having tried to enlist with the French Army in 1939, the de Gaullist "Free French" forces in 1940, the Canadian Air Force in 1941, and having been rejected by all of them because of his nationality, Walter Bodlander, 21-year old German refugee, at last has had his wish granted.

Today he has left to fight in the United States Army against the fascism which he so detests. Like all other aliens, Walter is not allowed to choose the branch he would like to serve with, but it doesn't matter to him as long as he has a go at the Fascists.

For months, Walter had been agitating for this country to declare war on the Axis, conducting practically a one-man war himself.

Those who knew Walter will remember him best by the story of how he got kicked out of the Senator Wheeler-America First meeting at the Olympic Auditorium. In fact, for a day he was the anonymous hero of the metropolitan press, which reported him merely as an "unidentified" young man who had been ejected from the fight stadium for attempting single-handedly to break up Senator Wheeler's meeting. Here's how it happened.

GRABS LEAFLETS

Walter, alarmed at the number of people who flocked to hear the Montana appeaser, grabbed up a stock of leaflets calling for all-out aid to Britain, China and Russia and began passing them out. Not content with peddling them outside the auditorium, he soon had worked his way inside.

An usher ejected him, warning that leaflet distributions were not permitted on the premises, but Walter thought that it would do no harm—on the contrary, that it would do good, because those on the outside of the auditorium were being bombarded with the anti-Semitic, pro-Nazi dodgers that were always to be found at America First meetings.

So Walter avoided the menacing usher and worked his way up to the balcony of the huge stadium. He had to work fast now, because the meeting would start soon. Suddenly, he got a brilliant idea. Instead of passing the leaflets out singly, why not shower them down from the balcony on the audience below? He had a good-sized bundle left, so he cut the string and let it go.

'LIKE SEAGULLS'

"They looked beautiful," he told his friends later, with delightful naivete. "The air was white with them, leaflets wheeling like seagulls."

Not so beautiful were the looks of the Fascists and the anti-Semites in the audience attracted by the spectacular display and connecting the tall thin boy standing at the balcony rail with the leaflets calling for the destruction of Hitler.

Born in Germany in 1920, Walter lived the 15 years until the Hitler scheme of things made itself manifest in unadulterated terror. Being both Jewish and anti-Nazi, his parents thought it best to send Walter to Switzerland; fortunately, they had the means to do so. In Lausanne, he received a typically French education, a desire to see France.

He arrived in Paris the day before war broke out, and sought to enlist in the French Army, only to find himself received with suspicion because of his nationality. He stayed there long enough for the French officials' apathy to impress itself on his mind.

"It seemed strange that the French should be digging their air raid shelters after war had broken out, instead of before," he says.

Given the choice of departure or a concentration camp, he left France for Palestine.

SINKING OF PATRIA

In Haifa, Walter witnessed one of the early tragedies of the war, the sinking of the French ship Patria, crowded with Jewish refugees.

Collected in Central Europe, the refugees had been traveling for six months on two months' provisions in an old tub. Arriving in Palestine in a state of indescribable squalor, they were refused permission to go ashore, were transferred to the Patria, because of the unseaworthy condition of their own boat. Ashore, a general strike was called in protest to the refugees' treatment by Palestinian authorities.

The night it was scheduled to sail for Madagascar, the Patria was sunk without warning in the harbor. The refugees were all below deck, having been ordered there by their Palestinian guards, so that they would not be able to witness the demonstration being staged on shore in their behalf. Instead of the two hours' time it would normally take such a ship to sink, the boat sank in five minutes. More than 175 refugees were drowned.

Walter left Egypt in December, 1940, bound for the United States aboard the ill-fated liner Zam-Zam, which was torpedoed and sunk off the Brazilian coast on its return trip. In fact, the Zam-Zam encountered the raider on its voyage across, but managed to elude it, Walter says.

Arriving here in February, Walter received his first citizenship papers in May. The rest is fairly contemporary history — about his "one-man" crusade to get the United States to declare war on Germany. He's still sore that it had to be the other way around, Germany declaring war on the United States.

"But the thing to do is to get in there fast and finish off what they started," he says.

WALTER BODLANDER
got in there fast

Walter as captain, 1945

Left: Article about Walter's enlistment in the U.S. Army which followed immediately after the U.S. entered the war when the Japanese attacked Pearl Harbor. *People's World*, Los Angeles, January 27, 1942.

3

Some of the women mentioned in the autobiography—
dreams of futures together that never were to be.

1. Jannette in Neuchatel, May 1939.
2. Norma, AKA Nana, 1947.
3. The girl whom Walter met on the train to Marseilles
and with whom he spent several days until successfully
persuading her to return to Switzerland before the war broke out.
Name since forgotten.

TOP SECRET - BIGOT   N E P T U N E

BWM/jje

HQ RCT 8
APO 4, U S Army
211200B May 1944

FO No. 1

> Maps: FRANCE, 0808 4250, Scale: 1/50,000. Sheets 5E/2,
> 5E/4, 5E/6, 6E/1; 6E/3 & 4 6E/5, 6E/6,
> 5F/2 & 6F11.
>
> FRANCE, 0808 4347, Scale: 1/25,000. Sheets 34-18NW,
> 34-18SW, 34-20SW, 31-21 SE, 21-18NE, 31-18SE.
>
> Reference: FO No. 1 and Annexes thereto, Hq 4th Inf Div,
> 12 May 1944.

1. a. Enemy situation - Annex No. 2 (Intelligence).

    b. 4th Infantry Division, reinforced, on D-Day at H-hour
       (1) Lands on TARE (GREEN) and UNCLE (RED) beaches in column
           of regiments in the order of 8th Infantry, 22d Infantry,
           12th Infantry, 359th Infantry.
       (2) Assaults and breaches German defenses in UTAH area.
       (3) Seizes a beachhead to cover the landing and advance inland
           of the remainder of the VII Corps.
       (4) Captures CHERBOURG (1020) in conjunction with the 90th
           Infantry Division.

    c. Naval Task Force 125 provides lift, protection at sea, naval
       gunfire in support of the assault, and naval gunfire on call
       ashore and will breach underwater obstacles.

    d. IX Tactical Air Command furnishes air support for 4th Infantry
       Division.

    e. 101st Airborne Division lands at H-4 hours on D-day, seizes
       the western exits of the inundated area between ST MARTIN
       DE VARREVILLE (4098) and POUPPEVILLE (4393) both inclusive,
       secures CARENTAN (3984) and protects the south flank of the
       4th Infantry Division generally along the DOUVE RIVER east
       of ST. SAUVEUR LE VICOMTE (1994), destroys bridges north of
       CARENTAN at 365872, 382865, 419873, and 427876, seizes and
       defends from destruction dam at 397868, seizes STE MERE EGLISE
       and crossings over MERDERET RIVER at 315957 and 321930,
       Crossings over DOUVE RIVER at 309910 and 269928 will be
       destroyed by 101st Airborne Division after it is relieved
       in 4th Infantry Division Sector.

Invasion orders for the 4th Infantry Division for landing in Normandy, France.
First page.

Top: Hemingway and IPW Team 34 interrogating a German prisoner. Left: Captain Galvin, center, Hemingway. July 1944.

Bottom: Hemingway with U.S. staff officers in Normandy before the Breakout in Normandy; July 25, 1944.

Walter interrogating a wounded prisoner, July 1944.

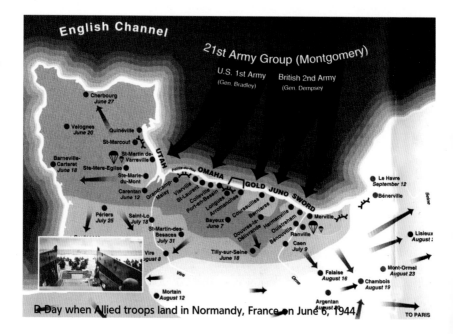

D-Day when Allied troops land in Normandy, France on June 6, 1944.

IPW Team 34 display a Nazi flag they had captured, 1945.

Munich, May 1945

France - July 25, 1944   13

Mr. Lee Payne
City Editor
The Daily News
Los Angeles, Calif.

Dear Lee —

It may be a long, long time before you read this letter, as it is being written at the front in   on this noisy and spectacular day which may turn out to be one of the historic dates of the war.

At any rate, I have made a friend here — the bearer — Lieut. Walter Bodlander, of Los Angeles, who wants desperately to be a newspaperman after the war. He has no entree at all — so I told him this would get him through your front door, and after that it's between you and him.

He is of German birth, an American now by citizenship and every inclination, and lived in Los Angeles before the Army. He is a prisoner-of-war interrogator, and doing a beautiful job. He is well-educated and highly intelligent. He can tell you the rest. Maybe I'll see you long before this note is handed to you. Hope so anyway. Best of all.

Ernie Pyle

Ernie Pyle's letter recommending Walter for a job as journalist. Pyle was killed soon after he wrote the letter and Walter never used it. Locations were cut out by the censor.

Walter with Ingrid Bergman and Jack Benny who were on a USO tour in Germany to entertain the troops shortly after the end of World War II.

Hitler's retreat, the "Eagle's Nest," in Berchtesgaden in the Alps shortly after the German surrender in 1945. The location of several international conferences, this was where Hitler summoned the Austrian premier before the "Anschluss" (March 1938). Walter visited the location with the idea of bringing home a souvenir.

By the time he arrived, others had completely stripped the place. Nothing was left— no furniture, no light bulbs, not even a doorknob.

19

Stranger even than the God's capricious decisions are the army's ideas of what to do with its soldiers: An order came from Corps headquarters: Every regiment was to send their mess officer and a mess sergeant to Cooks and Bakers School in Chattanooga. So once again, I was relieved from field duty and on my way to this weird assignment.

There were about 70 of us who arrived in Chattanooga—about 20 officers, the rest sergeants and corporals. We were met in a conference room at the Reed House, the largest and finest hotel in town. A sergeant greeted us and explained he was in charge of proceedings.

"The officers," he said, "will be quartered in the hotel, the enlisted personnel at a nearby army base. The course will last four weeks. Classes begin at 7:30 a.m. and end at 6 p.m. Sundays and evenings are off and passes can be arranged. We will meet here tomorrow morning. The enlisted personnel will now assemble downstairs for transportation to the base.

As the room emptied, the sergeant resumed his instructions. The officers' day will start at 9 a.m. with classes until noon. There will be a lunch break and the afternoon starts at 2 p.m. and will be used for field inspections of various kitchens. The day will end at 5 pm." The poor fellow did not get much further. He was interrupted: "I'm

Colonel X, ranking officer here, and I will decide on the schedule for the officers. Classes will be held from 10 to noon, Monday through Thursday. Afternoons are free. Field inspections of kitchens will be limited to one per week on Monday afternoons. I presume the first class will start tomorrow morning at 10 o'clock. Unless there are any questions, you are dismissed." Thus began my four weeks (paid) vacation in Chattanooga.

Frankly, I remember nothing of the classes. Probably, they covered food sanitation. Anyway, with so much free time I began to meet some of my fellow officers and, thus, made friends with Jim, a fellow second lieutenant who was a young confident guy— outgoing, witty and excellent company. My strong accent still bothered me a lot and I did not feel I could mingle with Tennessee locals. Jim spent most of his evenings at the Reed House Bar and eventually persuaded me to join him.

"I don't know anybody," I protested. "Neither do I," said he, as we settled at a table. "Just watch." He went to the bar where four or five girls were sitting, tapped two of the best-looking ones on the shoulder and said: "You and you, follow me." To my utter amazement, they did and sat down at our table. We had a pleasant evening together. Not much happened. Eventually Jim and one of the girls disappeared and I went back to my hotel room.

Now I have to admit that it was not just our charm that led to this easy conquest. By 1942 most young men were in the Army and the girls had a hard time finding suitable companionship. In addition, Chattanooga girls were particularly disadvantaged because close by was Camp Oglethorpe, the first WAAC (Women's Auxiliary Army Corps) base and these girls got frequent passes to Chattanooga. That made the city a young man's paradise.

But when you're shy, you're shy. And I remained uncommitted. Until... Until one Sunday afternoon when Jim said: "Let's go to a party."

"What do you mean? What party?"

"Just come with me."

At the hotel elevator, he said: "Name a floor."

I chose "7". On the seventh floor, we got out and walked

through the corridor. Music came from several rooms and a good number of doors were open, over-spilling with partygoers. "Come here, lieutenant."

An arm reached out and I was pulled into a room. Dance music, liquor, laughter, crowded happiness and at my side, my captor, the most beautiful WAAC, handing me a drink.

"So, who are you and what's this funny accent?" I tried to explain but the noise of some 20 men and women partying in a small hotel room made all communication virtually impossible. The radio was playing "I'll Be Seeing You"—one of the most popular tunes at the time and this gorgeous creature was singing in my ear, swaying with the music. The bourbon in my glass, the perfume she wore, the sudden intimacy, being pressed close to one another in this room charged with sexual energy was totally intoxicating.

We exchanged names, tried to talk, but the din was too much to take.

"Finish your drink and let's get out of here," my WAAC suggested, and just as she had pulled me into the room, she now pulled me out.

"How about some dinner downstairs?" It was more of a command than a question.

Thus began my relationship with Norma. She was 22, strikingly beautiful, even in army uniform and exuded the self-confidence many super beautiful women pretend to possess. To her, it came naturally. That first dinner was one of many to follow and it set the tone for the next two weeks. I fell head over heels in love with her while she was intrigued, amused, flattered, attached to me, yes, but totally in control.

I called her "Nana", and I was "Frenchy" to her. Her perfume was "Toujours Moi"—a fitting choice, both in scent and name. Over time, our relationship intensified but the dynamic never changed. I was in love; she was in command. To me, she was the American idol. Everything about her seemed exotic. She told me about her home town in the South, how she grew up, got married—"Yes, I'm married"—became a nightclub singer in

Atlanta, filed for divorce and in an impetuous and patriotic impulse joined the WAAC, while waiting for her divorce to become final...

I told her about Europe, Neuchatel and Jeanette and amused her with stories—true and false. She was stationed at nearby Camp Oglethorpe, got evening passes almost nightly and, of course, on weekends. Most evenings Nana sang the songs of the 30s to me in her sultry sexy voice—songs I had never heard but began to love. "Sophisticated Lady" and "Why Don't You Fly Right" were among my favorites. She would cuddle up close and sing them in a very low voice into my ear.

"That's how we met, don't forget," she would say and stop. I would beg for more but to no avail. "Time to eat," she would smile sweetly and seductively and that was that. Nana was in control and that included sex.

One evening we had rented a car and drove to Lookout Mountain, a romantic spot, not too far from Chattanooga. We were having dinner at a garden restaurant overlooking the city, sitting next to each other, holding hands. Dessert had been served and eaten. Nana was softly singing into my ear. I was in heaven and very anxious to get back to our room. Nana, I suppose was not in the mood for sex that night. "Not yet," she said. "Let's have one more drink."

We ordered our third bourbon—more than I could handle, but Nana had no trouble holding her liquor. She used it as her favorite weapon and it always worked. By the time we were ready to leave, I was out of it. She drove us home. Needless to say, there was no sex that night.

In wartime, nothing is permanent. It all came to a crashing halt when my "school" ended. I reported back to my Unit, which was still on maneuvers, and Nana continued her military adventure. That, however, did not last long. As soon as her divorce came through, she applied and received a discharge and went back to Atlanta. We began a correspondence. I pined for her. She replied with cheerful, crazy stories of her life. My Unit's maneuver consisted of a war game somewhere in the plains of

Oklahoma. We were the Red team—our object: to find and destroy the opposing Blue army. Officers from a neutral division acted as arbiters. We had been at this for several months but evidently we just did not get it right. The maneuvers continued.

20

Just before the Cooks and Bakers order, I had met a fellow officer, who in civilian life was a German Lit professor at Harvard. This week, he said, was his last week at this shitty maneuver. He had applied for a transfer to Military Intelligence some time earlier and his new assignment had just arrived. He suggested that I, too, should apply.

"You'd be far more useful to the war effort than what you are doing now."

That made sense, and so I, too, applied. Knowing the ways of the Army, I did not expect much. It was far too sensible an idea and would probably not be acted upon. So I continued my duties as Forward Observer, flew over the "battlefield", slept uncomfortably in tents and dreamed of Nana and the days in Chattanooga. The daily routine was boring and uneventful. "Hurry up and wait"—the time-honored motto of the military, was the order of the day.

Then came a sudden and unexpected change: Second Lieutenant Bodlander was to report immediately to Army Headquarters back in Camp Forrest. The order was stern and ominous. I asked my commanding officer what was going on. He seemed baffled but sympathetic. "You have been reported AWOL (absent without leave) and they are preparing a possible court martial. But don't worry, it must be a mistake, we know where you were at all time." At Army Headquarters, the tone was guardedly friendly. "We have obtained the daily roster from your division and you are reported as present, but somehow we have this request from Washington to investigate your status. You will have to stay here until we can explain what is going on."

It took just one day to unravel the mystery. About four weeks earlier, orders had been issued by the Military Intelligence Center that my application for transfer had been received and approved. I was to report immediately to Camp Ritchie for training and assignment. Since the order came from Military Intelligence, it was classified "Secret". A large red SECRET stamp was affixed to the top of the document and the receiving clerk at my regiment promptly stacked it away into the vault for "Secret Documents" and that is where it remained. No one saw it, certainly not me—a mere Second Lieutenant. Thus, the order to report to Camp Ritchie never reached me.

During the war, document classification was taken very seriously. There was "Confidential," "Secret," "Top Secret" and the highest "Top Secret Bigot". The Normandy invasion orders carried that designation. I suppose one cannot blame the regimental clerk too much for hiding away the secret order although, obviously, he should have shown it to his commanding officer. Later at Camp Ritchie I learned that the purpose of intelligence agencies is to gather information but never to pass it on. Information is power, so why share it. CIA, FBI and other agencies learned this lesson fast. Control is everything.

I might add that when in combat this attitude changed. The information that I and others at all levels gathered was freely disseminated to all who needed to know. The power game takes place only in the offices and bureaucracies where people believe they are not in immediate danger.

I left Camp Forrest, grateful to escape maneuvers. My directions were to take the train to Baltimore, then to change to a small local railway into the Blue Ridge Mountains. I was to get off at Huntsville, the code name for Camp Ritchie, where an agent would meet me. I was cautioned never to mention the secret training center by name. It was late afternoon and the train was full of commuters going home from work in Baltimore. When the ticket collector came through the compartment, I asked him how long it would get to Huntsville.

"Don't worry," he said, "I'll let you know." And, indeed, after an hour or so, he strolled through the car and called out: "Next stop, Huntsville, Camp Ritchie Military Intelligence Training Center." So much for secrecy!

As I was reporting several weeks late, the assignment for which I had been chosen had already filled. It was evidently a very secret affair because I was never told what it was. At the time, we were dropping agents and supplies into France to help the Maquis and FFI (both underground guerilla French organizations), and I suspect my assigned job had to do with such a mission. Anyway, rather than sending me back, I was assigned to the training unit for interrogation of prisoners of war.

Camp Ritchie was a military base unlike any other I had ever seen or heard of. Located in the hills of Maryland along a beautiful lake, not far from Hagerstown, before the war it had been a Country Club for the very wealthy and privileged. It was on a sprawling site of hundreds of acres and included a clubhouse with bar, dining room and about 20 guest rooms. A magnificent lounge, opulently furnished, faced the lake and small beach. Beautifully landscaped walkways led to the many cabanas in which we, the officers, were quartered—four to a cottage—each with our private bath and bedroom.

For years, FDR had used the place as his retreat, which he called Shangri-La. After the war, it was renovated and re-opened as Camp David.

Officers and enlisted personnel were segregated. Much later I learned that the accommodations and treatment at Ritchie were harsh and unpleasant for ordinary soldiers. In the segregated Army of World War II, unequal treatment was common. Sadly, I have to admit that I was completely unconcerned and probably unaware of the injustice of it all.

Ritchie was run by Colonel Banfil and was reminiscent of my

recent Cooks and Bakers School experience. The order of the day was: "Enjoy yourself."

Physical training was reasonable. Half an hour of calisthenics every morning, a three-mile march each day, and a 12-mile march once a week. Main classes were in techniques of interrogation, structure of the German Army, Order of Battle of the German Army and the SS, use of various "silent" weapons and some self-defense. Pretty basic stuff.

We had a lot of free time, which we spent mostly at the club-house bar. Everyone was allowed to make a reservation for a room at the club for weekends. Many of the higher-ranking officers were older and married, and they frequently invited their wives. Others just invited their current girlfriends. I invited Norma. Most of the girls from nearby Hagerstown sooner or later were guests at the lodge but Norma never came. She was urged, time and again, to come, agreed to do so, but never showed up. Fifty years later she told me that she remembers that my invitations were not "sincere enough". Bull!!

By order of the colonel, Fridays were Banfil Days—no duty, ushering in a three-day weekend. Banfil had some special connections at the War Department and he used them to great advantage. Whenever a chef from a major restaurant in the U.S. was drafted, he would wind up at Camp Ritchie in the Officers' Mess. With several world-renowned chefs in charge of the kitchen, we had extraordinary culinary experiences on a daily basis. The finest desserts crowned every meal. Baked Alaska—Banfil's favorite—was on the menu at least twice a week. Although each of us had to pay a small "contribution" to the Mess Fund, we all participated happily in this clearly illegal debauchery.

Many stories of intrigue and lust at Ritchie made the rounds. My favorite one concerned a local girl Mabel of Hagerstown. A frequently invited guest, one Saturday afternoon she was sitting in the lounge sipping a cocktail with a number of girls, who were waiting for their men. An officer had taken a nude swim in the lake. Noticing that the cocktail hour was already in progress and realizing he had only one towel at his disposal, he had to make a decision how to use it while crossing the lounge to get to his room. Drape the towel around his waist—or better, not to be recognized, put it over his face.

Decision made, he stumbled blindly through the room. "Thank God, it's not Harry," said one girl. "Glad it's not my husband," said another. "Not Billy," said a third. So went the comments. Mabel took a good look and said: "Hello!! There's someone new here at Ritchie!"

A good number of my fellow officers at Camp Ritchie were German Jews like me. As we marched on our daily exercises through the Maryland countryside, we sang songs we remembered from our Boy Scout days or songs from the German Army of World War I. We laughed at the irony of it all and, generally, had a good time during those last days of summer 1943.

21

I t was not such a good time for the Allies. Germany ruled all of continental Europe. Nazi armies had conquered the Romanian oilfields, had moved deep inside the Soviet Union, and were advancing steadily toward their ultimate goal—Caucasus oil. Stalingrad lay ahead—the last major obstacle to total German domination.

Of the many armies of Europe, only the Red Army was left to oppose the Nazi Wehrmacht. Beginning with the invasion of the Soviet Union in 1941, the Allies had been dedicated to help Russia with war materiel as much as possible. For months on end, Stalin pleaded for "real" help: an invasion of Europe, a Second Front— to force Germany into a two-front war and, thus, to relieve some of the pressure on the Red Army.

Churchill insisted that the West was not ready. Not in 1941, maybe in '42. Now we were in 1943. The West was fighting Germans in Africa and Italy but the promised and most meaningful Second Front in Western Europe did not materialize until June 1944. By then, 600,000 Germans had surrendered at Stalingrad, Soviet defeats had turned into Russian victories and the steady Soviet advances towards the German heartland assured the collapse of the Nazi armies.

Today, fueled by the unfortunate Cold War, we in the West give little credence to the amazing sacrifices of the Soviet people and the Red Army as they fought Germany, for months basically alone. At the time, of course, it was different. I remember the news reports in the Stars and Stripes (U.S. Army newspaper for the troops) when General Eisenhower referred to "the victories of our Soviet allies by the glorious Red Army". Certainly, the Western Allies helped to win the war. But the lions' share belongs to the USSR. Compare their civilian and military losses to ours, and you'll arrive at rather interesting conclusions.

Meanwhile back in 1943, I was enjoying Baked Alaska at Camp Ritchie. Then, in September, I got orders to report to Broadway, England, the Headquarters of U S Military Intelligence in Europe. Alone, but in the company of several thousand other soldiers I sailed on the Queen Mary (or, maybe, it was the Queen Elisabeth) to England.

The crossing must have been rather uneventful. I remember very little of it. The Queens were used to transport troops. They were very effective—crossing the Atlantic with considerable speed. They were faster than U-boats and, thus, the Germans never succeeded in attacking them.

The years 1942 and 1943 were the worst years for Allied shipping. German subs were prowling the oceans and, more or less, controlled the supply lanes to Britain. Henry J. Kaiser had started a new and successful enterprise. His naval yards were building "Victory Ships" rapidly and inexpensively. They were loaded with war supplies for England and the continent, but they were slow and had to sail in a convoy—six to eight together—escorted by anti-sub destroyers. Despite our vigilant navy, German subs sank these supply ships faster than Kaiser could build them.

Because the Queens could outrun any ship on the ocean, they sailed alone without escort. We docked at Firth of Clyde in Scotland. I had to report to HQ ETO (Headquarters, European Theater of Operations) in London to get instructions how to proceed to Broadway. This was my first visit to London. The city was bursting with energy. We saw the ruins caused by the Blitz— the German aerial attacks. Some streets were still blocked by rubble, but everywhere people were going about their business, not losing a beat. There was a feeling of contempt for danger in the air and a determination to get on with one's business.

In Germany as well, despite the incessant bombing, the population at large did not become demoralized and instead of rising against their own regime, as had been hoped, they became more defiant than ever. In the world of physics, we know that the more we compress a substance, the harder it gets. This holds true for people as well. Extreme force begets extreme resistance. Militarists the world over still don't understand that natural law: they're slow learners.

I was billeted in Grosvenor House, a luxurious hotel before the war, but at that time used to accommodate "unattached" officers. There must have been thousands of us: officers from all over the Allied world—Australians, French, Polish, Belgians, South Central and North Americans, British and French colonials and a host of others. They had been ordered to London for special duty or to await permanent assignments. Of course, only a few stayed at Grosvenor House, but all went there for food.

In the basement of the hotel was an enormous ballroom, which had been converted into a mess hall. As one descended the stairway, one came to a balcony-like landing, formerly used as a wardrobe, from which one could overlook the huge hall. Two wide, beautifully curved, sweeping staircases, one on each side, led to a cafeteria-like food table—the width of the entire ballroom.

Volunteer ladies were serving breakfast, lunch or dinner, depending upon the time of day. The rest of the gigantic room was filled with hundreds of small tables for us to sit and eat. The facility was open 24-hours a day and served about 500 meals an hour. An unending stream of men descended these stairs to the food line. I loved to stand on the balcony and watch the activity below.

Female volunteers—young and not so young—brought beverages around to the tables and cleared them as we finished. Though hundreds of men were in line at all times, one never had to wait, the line moved smoothly and the whole thing was a marvel of organization. This so impressed me that many years later on a visit to London I went back to Grosvenor House to see the "old officers' mess". No one at the hotel knew what I was talking about. I told them of the former ballroom in the basement.

"Oh, that! That was converted into an ice skating rink after the war, but has since been closed for many years. Now it's not used for anything."

I asked if it were possible to see it and they generously escorted me down. It was all still there, a little smaller than I had remembered—and not an Allied officer in sight.

Just before my European assignment, just before I would be leaving Camp Ritchie, I had been given a few days leave, which I used to visit my friend Goetz in Philadelphia. He, too, was now in the army and, by chance, was on leave as well. Together with his wife Lucy, we celebrated our reunion. In the course of the few days there, they introduced me to a friend of theirs—the lovely, beautiful psych student Albertine. It was what the French call a "coup de foudre" ("love at first sight"), evidently for both of us.

We spent the few remaining days of leave together without the benefit of Goetz and Lucy and dreamed happily of wonderful years together. We almost got married and only at the last moment realized the youthful folly of it. Not only did we hardly know each other but I was heading off to Europe and facing a very uncertain future. Together with our friends, we celebrated our engagement instead and promised eternal love. Gone were thoughts of Norma. Even Jeanette faded away.

I reported to Military Intelligence in Broadway, a small village in the center of England. Idyllic, quiet, untouched by the madness of the outside world, it managed to plod on in its timeless ways, undisturbed even by the sudden arrival of the Yanks. There were a few streets with mostly 18th century houses, two churches, a teahouse and, of course, a pub—the "Leg 'n Arms."

The American author J. D. Salinger—who I'm convinced was also in Military Intelligence—describes Broadway, or a similar little village in his short story, "For Esmé—with Love & Squalor". (For those of you who like to red short stories, this is a must.)

My stay in Broadway was very brief. Within a few days, I was given command of Interrogation of Prisoners of War Team (IPW) 34 and with my six men and two jeeps, we were off to Bath, England, where the 4th Infantry Division was stationed. From there I was assigned to the 8th Infantry Regiment at Exeter.

When I reported to my commanding officer Colonel James Van Fleet, I was greeted with extreme skepticism. As an "assigned" unit, my six men and I were not directly under his command. Theoretically, we were under orders from MI at Broadway.

"Just what are you here for? What are you supposed to be doing?" the colonel asked. I replied that our function was to interrogate prisoners as they were captured and to find out who the enemy forces were, how strong they were, to obtain locations of opposing machine gun nests and artillery positions and, in general, to assist in the tactical planning of the regiment. I also added that we intended to participate in all training and maneuvers with the regiment. Instantly, the tone changed and Colonel Van Fleet became a lasting friend and advisor. He introduced me to the G2, Major Todd, to whom I was to report our findings.

Walter Todd, too, became a long-time friend and on the occasion of the 50th anniversary of the invasion of Normandy in 1994, we spoke on the phone and exchanged photos.

The drive from Broadway to Bath and eventually to Exeter was beautiful and exhilarating. The English countryside seemed gloriously peaceful. We drove for many kilometers through open farmlands on narrow two-lane roads, occasionally passing through sleepy villages. There was barely any traffic. The vehicles on the road were either British or U.S. army trucks.

When we arrived at Devon, the landscape changed as we drove through the Dartmouth moors. It was towards evening. The sun was setting in a red glow and all around us were the undulating empty fields of the moor—an enchanting and haunting sight. We stopped our jeeps and sat in silence inhaling the untouched enormous wilderness. There was no sound, just the slight rustling of the wind. During my stay in Devon, I would often take a ride into the moors and each time I would gain strength and tranquility from that beautiful landscape.

Exeter was a busy little town with shops, theaters, movies and even a local ballet company. Like most towns in southwest England, it was swarming with American troops. The town showed some scars from previous air raids, but it had recovered quite well by 1943. During my stay there, we experienced no air attacks. My regiment was billeted in an old British army barracks at the edge of town. We were comfortably housed and began training immediately.

It was early September or October and on the second day after my arrival, we were informed that the regiment was designated an assault unit in the pending invasion of Europe. We would undergo rigorous invasion maneuvers. Strict discipline and secrecy was expected. Any breach would result in court martial.

The daily routine concentrated on physical fitness. Long marches were routine, often ending in obstacle courses where one had to crawl beneath a barbed wire installation while live machine gun fire overhead forced you to stay as low as possible. Since no one ever got hurt, we assumed that the "live ammunition" may not have been real, but no one wanted to take a chance!

Duty ended at 7 p.m. and everyone was allowed to go into town. Curfew was at 11 p.m. The local girls were far outnumbered by American soldiers. Draft-age English men were mostly away and only occasionally were they back home on short leave. There were a few English units around and we trained with some of them. Many had seen combat on the continent and were far more experienced than we were. We, on the other hand, were much better paid and better fed than our English friends who understandably envied us.

Relations were cool and best expressed in the very popular expression: "The problem with the Yanks is: They're over-sexed, overpaid, and over here."

I used to head into town to watch movies, eat at restaurants, and take in some theater. Of course, eventually I met a local lass— Ellie. She was married to a lieutenant, who was stationed some- where in the Middle East. We hit it off right away but we both in agreed that out relationship had to be one of friendship and nothing more. We met almost every day and I became very fond of her. England had clearly adapted to war. Overhead in Exeter were the barrage balloons. These Zeppelin-shaped balloons, about 150 feet long, were anchored to the ground by steel cables. They drifted about 1,000 feet up, hundreds of them, in and around the city. They were installed to prevent German aircraft from low-level bombing raids and they were very effective.

At night, everything was blacked-out. Car lights were dark blue, enough to see a vehicle but not enough to help driving it. With no streetlights, every one drove very slowly and carefully. All windows were curtained so that no light would escape. To enter a shop, one had to go through several sets of dark curtains before opening the door.

To minimize mass casualties from air raids, all of England was on "British Double Summertime". Clocks were set two hours ahead. Restaurants started serving dinners at 6 p.m. (in reality 4 p.m.) and closed by 10 (actually 8 and still daylight). Theaters and movies began their last performances at 7 p.m. (5 p.m.) and conclude by 9 p.m. (7 p.m.) so that everyone could return home before dark and be back in familiar territory in case of a nighttime air raid.

Everything was rationed. Everyone had ration books or coupons, even us soldiers. Everything was in short supply but, of course, we had much more access to goodies than the civilian population so I was happy to be able to give my lady friend little gifts. We had a PX (Post Exchange), an Army-run general store— where we could buy all kinds of luxuries from bananas and oranges to nylons, none of which were available in civilian stores.

Both Ellie and her husband survived the war and for a long time afterwards, I received letters from them, including photos of their baby. In the U.S., at war's end, we were comfortable but we knew how hard life was for many of the people living in Europe. There were shortages of everything, including basic foodstuff. Ellie's letters never asked for help but the need was evident. To this day, I'm still ashamed that I gave so little assistance to my friends. Other than an occasional CARE package, not much else.

Though I was broke, I should have done more. Millions of CARE packages were sent to Europe between 1946 and 1950. They contained meat, butter, rice and other much-needed nutrients, each package weighing about 20 pounds. "Spam" was one of the ingredients and became a European favorite. Hundreds of thousands of people were thus saved from starvation.

22

Actual invasion training began two weeks after my team arrived in Exeter. It started with intensive lectures on the workings of combustion engines and their inability to function when submerged in saltwater. Diagrams of every kind of vehicle—from jeeps to tanks—were presented and those parts of the engines outlined which needed to be waterproofed.

Then came the "hands-on" drill. Every officer and enlisted man had to become expert on how to apply the stuff necessary to waterproof the vehicles and to learn how to remove it. The waterproofing material was a greasy, oily, honey-colored paste with the consistency of cream cheese. Once the engines were covered with that stuff, a stiff hose was attached to the exhaust pipe and raised to extend two feet above the expected waterline. Vehicles had to be able to function completely submerged, with water up to, and above, the steering wheel.

It took well over 30 minutes to prepare a car properly and it was a very messy job. But the main emphasis was on the speedy and complete removal of the waterproofing. Because water-proofed engines would overheat and could not be driven very far with all that stuff on them, it was essential to get them back to their original condition. Obviously, that would eventually have to be done at the beach, after landing and under fire. Speed was of the essence. To waterproof all vehicles and then, after inspection, to remove the stuff became a daily routine.

While preparing for invasion maneuvers, all leaves were cancelled. No one was allowed into town. There could be no contact with civilians.

Then came the order: waterproof the vehicles. A few hours later the whole regiment began the slow drive to Exmouth. At the harbor we were sent to designated areas where we waited for hours, finally to be loaded into various invasion crafts, in my case an LCVP (Landing Craft, Vehicle and Personnel) which held two jeeps and 12 men.

As soon as everyone was safely onboard, we were ordered to disembark, remove the waterproofing and drive back to Exeter. This was my first maneuver and I remember it so clearly because we all thought that this was "the real thing"—the beginning of the invasion.

What a disappointment! A week later there was a second maneuver—very similar to the first but this time, we went out to sea and after circling for hours and waiting for the whole flotilla to assemble, we landed on an isolated—obviously friendly— beach. We learned the name of that place was Slapton Sands, somewhere in western Devon. From October through May, we assaulted Slapton Sands endlessly. Sometimes at night, sometimes in stormy weather, and since we were never told what our mission was, we always assumed that this time would be the real thing.

Each exercise was clearly designed to make us think that we were about to go into combat, especially when a new or a more persuasive detail was added. Live ammunition was issued, next time we all got First Aid kits. Finally, prior to the start of one exercise, we were told to pack all our belongings into a footlocker with our home address on it to be sent back to the U.S. However, each time we ended up at Slapton Sands.

The LCVP—a landing craft—was an oversized rowboat. It was open—about 10 ft. wide, 36 ft. long, with side walls about 5 ft. high, and the front flap about 7 ft. high. It was commanded by a navy officer, who had no idea where we were to land. His orders were to wait for a radio signal while at sea, and then to open an envelope, which would tell him how to proceed and where to steer the boat..

These pilots could use their own discretion to determine how close to the shore they would steer their craft before lowering the flap. Most of the time they were willing to get us quite close to the beach and, generally, we would wade ashore in water no higher than our knees.

An exception came in March 1944. The whole regiment was loaded onto a large troop ship and transported north to Scotland. There, at high sea, we were transferred into waiting LCVPs. The boats immediately moved toward the shore and stopped. When the flap was lowered, it was evident that we would just barely be able to touch ground to wade ashore.

We complained but the naval officer explained that this was precisely the purpose of the exercise. We were to be completely drenched and once on the beach, we were to wait for trucks to pick us up about five hours later. Meanwhile, we were to keep ourselves as fit and as warm as possible without building a fire. It was an overcast March day in Scotland with the temperature—probably in the low 50s. I remember it as one of my more miserable experiences in the Army. Fortunately, no one in my Unit got sick.

After April, our port of embarkation was changed to Plymouth. We went through many more maneuvers. Each time as the long convoys would wind their way through town to the harbor, the population barely paid attention to us. It had become so routine—both to them and to us. On many of these maneuvers, we had been at sea for hours before the signal to land was given. However, each time, we landed at Slapton Sands.

Yes, Slapton Sands became a familiar beach and always, it was a disappointment. We were ready for action. We knew there was danger ahead but the knowledge that we were going to play an important—even historic—role in this war was so intoxicating that it allowed no room for fears. Sometime, in the middle of May we again received the order: "Waterproof the vehicles." Leaves into town were cancelled as usual, but this time we were told that no letters could be mailed home.

This was news. And it was also news that absolutely nothing was happening the next few days. Nothing, We just sat there and waited. Then finally vehicles were lined up in convoy formation and we started to roll. Slowly, we drove through the beautiful and desolate moors of Devon. Then the column stopped and unit-by-unit, we were directed off the road into camouflaged fields. Each unit was guided into a specific area, fenced in with chicken wire and with camouflage nets overhead. Armed MP guards stood by the gates of each area. We were instructed to dismount, to be prepared to stay put for several days and not to leave the area unless we received specific permission.

On the second day, I was given a special pass and summoned to an enclosure where there was a huge tent. In the middle of the tent was an enormous table. A detailed relief map was spread out over the table. Regimental and battalion staff officers and company commanders gathered and then the briefing began.

First, we were led to a smaller table displaying a normal-sized map. This, we were told, was the Cotentin Peninsula of France. Cherbourg, our main objective, was at the top of the map. We were to land on two beaches: our Division, on "Utah" beach; the First Division, to our immediate left on "Omaha" beach. The landings would be about 60 kilometers south of Cherbourg.

The objective for the first day was to take the village of Sainte-Mère-Église, to relieve the paratroopers who had been dropped during the night and then to proceed to secure the road to Cherbourg.

Now the briefing officer took us to the large table. "This," he said, "is an exact replica of the landing place Utah beach. Take all the time you need to get familiar with the territory. Note the distance between the beach to the road to Sainte Mère, remember the location of the two windmills, the farmhouse, major trees. Notice the two German pillboxes, which we think will be destroyed by the bombing prior to landing. Make yourself very familiar with the terrain. We don't want you get lost after you land. Get your men off the beach as fast as possible. Units that follow will secure the landing site. Find the road to Sainte-Mère and capture the village as fast as possible. Detailed written orders will be issued tomorrow. Regular and area photomaps are available; take as many as you need.

"Now a few important words. No one is to drink the local water. You will be issued water for your canteens. It is important that all men know not to touch the water. If need be, you can drink wine or milk obtained from the farmers. Every man will be given 10 dollars worth of Invasion Franks. These are U.S.-issued bills. We will not honor the local currency. Try to stay on K-rations but if you want to buy local food, go ahead.

One more thing, pick up your morphine kit before you leave here. Every officer gets one kit with two ampoules: use the needles only under extreme conditions. Please ask any questions you wish. The entire day has been set aside for this briefing."

Of course, there were many questions but obviously the main one was: "When is D Day, when do we land? We were told that the day was not known. Period. Just as I was ready to leave the tent with all the maps and the invasion money, Colonel Van Fleet, the regimental commander came over and stopped me.

"Bodlander, you speak French and German, right?"

"Yes, sir."

"Well, I want you to be with me at the landing. We'll assign you to my LCVP," he smiled. "You'll be among the very first soldiers on French soil. Good luck!"

I liked Van Fleet. During training I had had very little to do with him, but he seemed fair and decisive. He had been a classmate of Eisenhower, the Supreme Commander at SHAEF (Supreme Head-quarters Allied Expeditionary Forces). Almost all of his classmates had been promoted to higher ranks. Van Fleet was one of the few who was "only" a colonel. It had been an oversight and now he wanted to make sure to be noted and remembered. So he saw to it that his would be leading regiment of the invasion.

By the way, it worked very well for Van Fleet. Within two months after the invasion, he was promoted to General, became a Division commander, and kept steadily rising in rank both during and after the war. Truman put him in charge of the American involvement in Greece and Turkey in the late 40s.

We stayed for a few more days in the fields of Devon. The weather was bad. It was cool and rainy. There was fog every morning.

23

Then, on June 4th, about noon we began to move. Slowly the column rolled towards the embarkation port at Plymouth—just as it had so many times before. But this time, as we entered the town, the sidewalks were crowded with people, waving and throwing flowers. From the windows, we heard cheers and shouts of "Good luck!" At every turn, people ran up to the convoy, waving and applauding. It was a very emotional send off. How did they know that this time it was the real thing? To this day I still wonder about that. Fortunately, the news did not spread to the Germans.

Van Fleet's LCVP contained his jeep, his small staff, and my eight men. By 3 p.m. we were at sea. The weather was miserable. It was raining. Everyone was drenched and cold. The craft circled in the ocean, presumably waiting for the whole force to assemble. We were on British "Double Summer Time", which meant it did not get dark until 10 p.m. and we hoped we would land in daylight. Now, it was already past midnight, but there was no shore in sight.

The ocean became rougher, the waves higher, the rain heavier. I tried to keep dry by crawling under a jeep but to no avail. The waves had splashed into the LCVP. The steel floor was totally wet. There came a moment when I didn't even try to keep dry any more. I was resigned to be drenched and cold and somehow this helped to accept the misery. Dawn came, no change in the weather, no word as to when we would begin our assault. The next day, June 5th went by... very slowly.

Everyone was now totally miserable and many were seasick. Occasionally, we heard planes overhead, presumably bombers on their way to France. We began to wonder if this was just another maneuver. But then about 4 a.m. on June 6th, our navy pilot told us that he had just received a signal to prepare for the assault.

H-hour was to be at 6 a.m. Now I was so excited that all fear was pushed out of consciousness. I remember two thoughts: "Thank God, we are landing," and "I'm making history".

It was still too dark to see the shore, but we could hear more bombers overhead and eventually as we approached land, we could see the flashes of exploding bombs in the distance. Other assault craft—to the right and left of us—were barely visible. As dawn was breaking, we were steaming towards the beach. The heavy guns of our Navy—which we had heard all night—were now silent. The only noise was the engine of the LCVP and the distant explosions from our aerial bombardment.

There was not a single German plane in the air. With Colonel Van Fleet, the assault commander, on board, the Navy pilot brought our craft as close to the shore as possible. When the flap was lowered, we moved onto the beach without even getting our shoes wet. We found no resistance, no enemy soldiers, and just a few artillery shells. I was trying to orient myself, but everything around me was confusingly strange—no windmills, no trees, no road in sight. Everything was different from what we had expected.

"Get off the beach" had been the order. So I climbed a not-very-steep dune and found myself in a field. Major Todd, my G-2 (Intelligence) commander was next to me. But where were we? No idea. Now mortars begin to hit our area. They were like artillery except that one could not hear them coming until just before they exploded. I still had not seen a single German soldier. Now we came to a road and a few meters further, there was a crossroads. Todd had his map out and tried to decide which way to go. Van Fleet came up and started yelling: "Don't stop at a crossroads. The enemy has his artillery trained on crossroads. Move a few meters away. By then, several companies had landed around us. We were about to move straight ahead when someone yelled: "Turn left. It's flooded up ahead."

Artillery and mortars were starting to rain down on us. Then the first jeep came up from the beach. It was Jim Moore and his men— the Communications platoon. They laid wires for field phones, which enabled the commanders to talk with their platoon leaders.

Lt. Moore was as confused as the rest of us. The jeep stopped at the crossroads to decide which way to go and got hit by a mortar. Jim lay there moaning, his belly open, one arm twisted, blood all around. His two men were dead, having been thrown from the jeep.

I could not tell if Jim was feeling pain or not, but he was lying there moaning, so I used my morphine on him and left him there. I assumed the medics would come soon to evacuate the wounded. The rest of the day was a blur of fear and confusion. In the afternoon, Todd told me that we had made contact with our parachute forces in Sainte-Mère-Église.

By now the first few German prisoners had been evacuated to the beach—just 500 yards behind us. So I went back to interrogate them. The scene at the beach was total chaos. I finally found a ragged bunch of very frightened German soldiers—14 of them— guarded by two GIs who didn't know what to do with them. We were all scared and had no way to protect ourselves from incoming shells. The prisoners were supposed to be sent back to England but, of course, there was too much confusion, so no one knew how or when this was supposed to happen.

Meanwhile, throughout all the noise and madness, I pulled out a bit of information from them. They were Landsturm (3rd Class militia)—an auxiliary and over-aged unit—and were expecting reinforcements in a few weeks. That was about it. Chronologically, I remember very little about those first days in Normandy. I can recall specific incidents, but day-to-day events are lost in the fog of distant times. I do remember the first night of the landing. After interrogating the prisoners on the beach, I was to return to my Unit, but I lost my way. By then, it was pitch black and raining. Climbing the dunes in the dark, I stumbled on a hedgerow and decided to wait out the darkness right there hoping to find shelter in the shallow ditch of the plants. Just to have a few branches of brush over me seemed better than nothing. Mortar and artillery shells were bursting constantly all around me, but the machine gun fire had stopped.

I had not slept since we had left England and now I realized how exhausted I was. Despite the rain, the cold, and the enemy fire, I must have dozed off in the depth of darkness. Suddenly, I felt someone next to me. A German soldier? Lying in the muddy ditch with my pistol in my hand and half asleep, I had no idea what to do. Then I heard the whisper: "Is that you, Lieutenant?" and realized it was Johnny Bear, my driver. Scared and shivering from the cold, he crawled down in the muddy ditch under the hedgerow. Well, we survived that night, but just barely.

The next day, the regimental command post (CP) was established and we began to sort out our situation. We had now established a provisional beachhead of about 1 square mile. Behind us, another division was about to land. The front was some 200 yards ahead of us. Sainte- Sainte-Mère was now in our hands.

Someone had dug an enormous foxhole, at least six feet deep, 10 feet wide and long. That was the regimental CP (Command Post). It remained there for the next few days. German prisoners were still being evacuated to the beach and, thus, I made several trips daily to the beachhead.

I remember returning from the beach, sitting at the CP, my feet dangling down, giving Major Todd beneath me the latest info I had received from the prisoners.

"By the way," I told him, "I'm surprised at how many bees there are here."

"What do you mean?" he asked.

"Well, every time I go to the beach and return back here, I

hear them buzzing all around me. I can hear them even now."

Todd laughed. "Those aren't bees, you idiot. They're machine gun bullets. You'd better get into a foxhole."

Luck? Destiny? Predestination? Who knows? For sure, I was extremely lucky many times during those next 12 months of war. In fact, the whole regiment was very lucky. The reason we were so confused at the landing was that the bad weather had pushed our Armada about a mile south of its intended destination. Had we landed on the planned beach, the reception would have been very different and far, far worse. The German pill boxes, which we had been told would be destroyed by the pre-assault bombing, were, in fact, very much intact. They held out for quite a few days and were finally neutralized by later landing units.

The farm fields of Normandy were bordered by stone walls or more frequently by hedgerows. These hedges, which had given me some comfort the first night were a bane to our frontline soldiers. They grew to six feet in height, were very dense, and became an excellent cover for German machine gun nests. Every time we tried to advance, our men had to cross these fields with the enemy hiding behind the next hedgerow. It was extremely dangerous and I felt very lucky that I did not have to be at the very front at that time.

After the fifth day or so, just as we reached the outskirts of Montebourg, we heard that there was trouble at the beach. Bad weather had destroyed the temporary harbor facilities and supply ships could not land. We began to be short of ammunition and food. Plans for an attack on Montebourg were cancelled; morale plummeted. By now prisoners were interrogated at the command post and then evacuated to the beach, now about 2 miles back. Everyone, of course, wanted to know what was happening with our supplies.

At that point, one man, a 57-year-old retired soldier became our idol. He was General Roosevelt, son of president Teddy Roosevelt. He had volunteered to land with us and now, realizing the emotional need for information about the beach situation, he made it his job to provide us with as much accurate information as possible. Daily he went back to the beach to bring us the latest news. It was a dangerous trek, often under heavy fire. The news he brought often was not good, but he was always optimistic and always told us the truth. Armed with his gnarled walking stick and a pistol, he stopped to talk with every soldier he encountered. We all loved that man and were very upset when we learned later that he had died of a heart attack in July.

Soon things improved. Roosevelt brought good news from the beach, reinforcements were landing, quartermasters sent ammunition and my two jeeps. The next day one jeep got a direct hit but no one was hurt. In the course of the war, I lost three jeeps to artillery, and not one of our team was hurt in those incidents. Talk about luck!

The regiment was now again at full strength and ready for an attack. At that moment, word came from one of our companies at the front that German soldiers were in the field with a white flag. Major Todd thought I should go and investigate. Now, the German soldiers I had interrogated so far had all been very discouraged. They knew of their armies' defeats at Stalingrad and in Africa, and their morale was extremely low. So, as I was rushing to the front, I was thinking: Maybe they want to give up. Maybe I could negotiate a major surrender. Already, I could see the headlines: WAR ENDS IN NORMANDY. LT BODLANDER HERO OF THE DAY.

At the front I looked through the hedgerow at an empty field. No one was there. Well, where were the white flags?

"They had been there just a few minutes ago," the GI said.

Some time went by. Nothing happened. I now decided to go into the field waving a white undershirt hoping a German soldier would come out to discuss the surrender. The company commander wanted an "OK" from higher up. We called Todd on the field phone. He thought I was crazy but, finally, I convinced him to let me try.

So there I was in the field with my white flag, half way to the German lines when a soldier finally appeared from the other side.

I could see he was a sergeant. We stopped about three feet apart. I began by saying: "We can speak German. I hear you want to surrender."

He was silent. Then he said: "What?"

"Well, we saw your men in the field with white flags, not 10 minutes ago."

"Oh," he said, "we were trying to evacuate one of our wounded."

Now, it was my turn to say, "Oh."

After some silence, I went on: "The war is kind of lost for you guys. Maybe surrender is a good idea."

"Well," he responded, "I'd have to talk to my Commander about that. It's not a bad idea but I can't act on this by myself."

So we agreed that he would talk to his captain and that we would meet again in five minutes. I phoned Todd and gave him the news. He was skeptical but said "Ok".

After a few minutes, I met the sergeant again. Yes, his captain thought surrender was a possibility but he must confer first with his Battalion Commander. They needed 10 minutes. I agreed.

We returned to our respective lines. Major Todd was not pleased. He told me we were preparing an attack. An artillery barrage was supposed to begin in five minutes. I had wasted half an hour already, he said.

"But I might be able to get a whole German battalion to surrender, maybe even a regiment. Give me a chance," I pleaded.

So I got another 10 minutes. The sergeant and I met again. Well, it was an important decision he told me. His officers wanted me to come to their command post for negotiations. They would give me an unconditional free pass through the German lines and promised to send me back if we could not agree. I told him I thought it was a great idea but that I needed permission from my superiors. We would meet in two minutes.

The headlines now read: WAR ENDS, BODLANDER A NATIONAL HERO.

On the phone, Todd was furious. "Permission denied. If you go, you will be listed as a deserter. Get your ass back here. Now! The regiment is scheduled for an attack and we're holding up the works. Artillery is ordered to start at one minute. Hear me, one minute!"

"The 12th infantry (our sister regiment) has already begun the attack to our right. They are two miles into German positions and we are sitting on our ass, waiting for you!" he yelled.

Finally, I got another five minutes from Todd to meet my sergeant. I went into the field immediately and he came out promptly.

"Deal is off," I told him, "but whoever wants to surrender right now, that's ok."

Will you take the wounded?" he asks.

"Yes, one for every two-able bodied men."

He wanted five more minutes. I told him we had no more time. "I'll wait here in the field for two minutes, then all is off."

A few moments later, the sergeant, two wounded soldiers and seven others surrendered.

Alas, no headlines!

Throughout all this time, the Germans had held their fire. Our artillery started almost immediately after I returned. Our attack was successful.

24

We captured Montebourg, and Van Fleet wanted to see the town and talk with the people. He called on me to accompany him. As we walked towards town on the unpaved main road, we noticed a few jeeps driving around a curve fast enough to create a dust cloud—a sure signal for enemy artillery to target the spot. So we decided to wait for the next jeep to station a soldier there to warn other vehicles to slow down.

Just as we were talking about this, several mortar shells exploded around us. When the barrage ended, I found myself in a ditch, blood running from my chest. Van Fleet had been thrown to the other side of the road. When I called to him, he said he was wounded, too.

Although I was bleeding profusely, I felt almost no pain. Soon a jeep came and took us to the field hospital. Of course, they wanted to attend to Van Fleet first, but he insisted that I should be the first to be looked after. It turned out that I had a very superficial wound. Shrapnel had hit my chest bone. The medics dug out the metal and a few splinters, dressed the wound, which by then was barely bleeding. Within two hours, I was released. Van Fleet had three pieces of shrapnel in his stomach. None had done serious damage. He was very lucky because one piece had stopped just short of his bladder. Had it pierced that organ, he probably would not have recovered. Turned out, he was released after a few days.

On the way to Cherbourg, after Valognes had fallen, two of our infantry companies needed to cross the main road. This was very dangerous because the area was under direct enemy observation and anyone crossing was subject to machine gun fire. Colonel Strickland, the assistant regimental commander, had made it his job to stand at the designated crossing point and warn every soldier to rush across as fast as possible. He himself went across back and forth several times, quite unnecessarily. I thought he was suicidal—determined to be wounded or killed in action—and, in fact, he was killed that day at that exact spot.

Cherbourg was captured by our sister regiment. The Germans had built heavy gun emplacements into the mountain range overlooking the town and harbor. They were connected by miles of tunnels. By the time I got there, the fighting was over. My eight men and I were assigned to guard the main entrance to the tunnel system and to prevent possible marauders or roving German units from re-occupying it. It occurred to me that this might have been a German headquarters and that important documents might well be found here. So I decided to explore the area.

Electricity had been knocked out, and except for an occasional sliver of daylight from the gun emplacements, the tunnels were pitch black. Armed with a flashlight, I went through this endless tunnel system. There were, indeed, many rooms there, but they all contained either ammunition boxes or canned food. Then I came upon a room stacked with burlap sacks, each evidently containing papers. I ripped a few open: they were full of freshly printed French money of all denominations. This was, of course, useless money since we knew the U.S. would not honor Vichy French currency. But for the hell of it, I stuffed my pockets with hundreds of thousands of French francs. All my men got some of the loot and from that time onward, we had plenty of play money for occasional cribbage and gin games.

Of course, I reported our find to Major Todd, who got his share of useless francs as well. All was not for naught, however. We found out that French farmers happily accepted our francs for whatever we wanted to buy. About two months later came our first payday. Unbelievably, we were paid in the very French currency we had so freely squandered. Major Todd told me that the Cherbourg cache had contained over 50 million dollars worth of Francs and the army had decided to use it, rather than to print new banknotes.

To add insult to injury, we were allowed to send our pay directly home to a bank of our choosing, and we could send any amount—even more than the pay. If only I had known! Alas, most of my francs had already been used in jest to light cigarettes. Since our GIs were ordered to take all money from captured prisoners, almost everyone sent more money home than they were paid. That wonderful loophole, however, was closed by the next pay period.

Day by day, the next 10 months of war have become somewhat murky in my memory. But a number of specific events remain as clear as ever and so do certain feelings and emotions. Fear is a constant—probably for every soldier on, or near, the front. Those who say they felt no fear have no imagination.

But fear did not paralyze us. It simply was an ever-present under-coating. Each time the front moved forward, I had to move; and with each move, I felt terribly uncomfortable. I had to leave a place where I had managed to survive for a day or two, and now I had to find a new and secure spot.

The horrible stench of death was constantly around us during those first three weeks. The heavy bombing prior to the invasion had killed hundreds of farm animals—mostly cows. The rotting carcasses now lay in the fields unattended and the horrific odor of decaying flesh permeated the air with a smell one can never forget.

The fields bordered by hedgerows often had stakes in them that looked like telephone poles. They were definitely not trees, nor could they be any crop—simply poles, about six feet high, planted upright and quite haphazardly throughout the fields. We wondered what they were for. It became clear a few days later when we were re-enforced by a glider company. The gliders, made of wood, had a wingspan of about 40 feet and held some 50 men.

As they came whooshing down at a speed of at least 60 miles per hour attempting to land in the fields, their wings would hit the poles. With broken wings at that speed, the disabled gliders crashed, twirling, spinning and tumbling—completely out of control. Many came to rest upside down. There were—to my knowledge—no fatalities but none of the men in the gliders were combat ready. Most had broken limbs; some had more severe injuries.

We had been in the fields when the gliders came down. There were at least 30 of them, coming in, and they seriously endangered our troops as they crashed around us. Luckily, few of us on the ground were hurt. The whole glider affair was a complete failure.

Thankfully, we had total control of the skies. I saw no German planes during the landing. Later a few of their fighters appeared and they created considerable damage and delay.

I'm certain that we would not have succeeded in Normandy had the Germans dominated the air. Lucky for us, the Luftwaffe was at that time fully engaged in Russia. After we had broken out of Normandy, a lone German plane would occasionally fly over the front, usually after dark. We dubbed him "Bedtime Charlie" and tried, unsuccessfully, to bring him down with 50-caliber machine gun fire. The red tracer bullets were like fireworks in the evening sky.

After those first days, I was never again directly at the front. I had to be near the regimental command post, generally two or three kilometers from the German lines. Although my unit, the IPW Team 34, had a machine gun and each of us had a rifle and I carried a pistol as well, I was never in hand-to-hand combat and with one exception, I never fired directly at the enemy.

That one exception was when I accompanied my friend David Rose, the Intelligence and Reconnaissance (I&R) platoon leader, on a mission to explore the front, which was quiet at the time. The mission was to try to engage the enemy, to test how strong they were and, if possible, to capture some prisoners. We ran into an enemy patrol and after a short fire fight disengaged and returned to our position. These missions were routine for the I&R platoon— luckily, not for me. My job was to interrogate prisoners.

25

The treatment of prisoners is much discussed these days because of the disgraceful attitude of the Bush administration carrying out unlawful interrogation methods. In WWII—on our side—the question of torture never came up. We knew the rules of the Geneva Convention and we adhered to them. That was that.

Interrogation of prisoners took place at various levels. At Corps and Army levels, far from the fighting, we were interested in strategic information: What was the morale at home? How did the city population react to the bombing? What were the future plans of the German army? Etc. At my level, at the front, we needed to know the location of machine guns and artillery installations? How tired or how fit were the units fighting against us? How recently had they been supplied with new equipment? Were we facing motorized units? In short, we needed tactical information that could help the companies at the front.

The prisoners sent to my unit were not wounded or only had superficial wounds. Usually, they had been captured less than 30 minutes earlier, and most of them were still in shock. With few exceptions, they were scared, and many believed they would be shot. As they arrived at my Unit, we separated them from each other immediately and would not allow them to speak with each other. Interrogation was always conducted one by one, and out of earshot of other prisoners.

Every German soldier was required to carry a "Soldbuch"—a pay book. It was an ID containing name, rank, serial number, and the name of the unit to which the soldier was assigned. It had a record of the pay he had received to date.

Prisoners were allowed to keep their personal papers, such as family pictures, letters—and their *Soldbuch*. Everything else was confiscated, mostly wristwatches, money, perhaps a knife, and endless trinkets. Of course, they had already been disarmed when they were captured.

The Soldbuch information was of great help to us. Trembling and disoriented, the prisoner would readily give his name but often did not want to give the name of his Unit. Of course, we already knew it; it was right there in the Soldbuch, and soon we also knew the names of the commanders of these units.

So a typical interrogation would go about like this:

"So, you won't tell me the name of your Unit? And you won't answer any more questions? Well, my friend, I know the answer to all these questions. What I don't know is whether you are going to cooperate or be difficult. And, of course, that will determine whether you live or die. Up to you.

"Now then: You are part of the 12th *Fallschirmjäger* Regiment and your commander is Hauptman Bensch. And you are a wireman. You were captured laying phone wires from the artillery to your CP."

By that time, most prisoners were amazed that we knew all that. Why did we ask him? We allowed a little time to let this sink in.

Then we would continue: "Ok, here is a map. Here is where you were captured. Now let's see if you want to live. Show me where you were captured... Ok, good. And where is your command post? Ok, now show me where you came from with your wires. How far back is the artillery?" Etc. etc.

Most of the time, those were sufficient questions to get very accurate information. Once in a while, someone would not cooperate. I remember a lieutenant who was particularly defiant. So after a number of unanswered questions, I called to one of my men.

"Sternberg," I said in German, "here's another one like Corporal Bauer (a prisoner from the same unit, whom we had just inter-

rogated). I've had it with these damn Nazis. Take care of Bauer."
Sternberg would disappear behind a tree or a shed and we would hear a couple of pistol shots. Sternberg would return and salute.

"Thanks, Sternberg."

"Now, lieutenant, let's try it again. It's your last chance to cooperate. But if you want to join Bauer, that's fine with me."

This kind of deception was not needed very often, but when used, it worked every time. In fact, we never harmed any prisoners but if necessary we sure did scare them. Most of them didn't seem to realize that we were speaking to them in German. They were still too traumatized from being captured and only a few remarked on my accent-free German.

A surprisingly large number cooperated freely, answered all questions and gave very useful information. Everything we learned went immediately to Todd. On a daily basis, we were expected to submit all findings in writing to the G-2.

26

With Cherbourg captured and the Cotentin secured, we heard that we would be sent home for a much-deserved rest. Alas, like most rumors, these stories turned out to be unfounded.

Instead, we moved on towards St. Lo and Coutances. British, Canadian and American forces had captured both towns and we were to hold the important road between them. It was late June—warmer, but still raining frequently. Suddenly, we received orders to withdraw from the very road we had just secured. No one was aware of any problems at the front, but all units moved back about three kilometers.

My regiment established headquarters in an abandoned farm. We had found a great spot. The main house was a 17th century stone building with more rooms than we could use. Soon however the building began to fill up. Jeeps arrived in the courtyard disgorging high-ranking officers, heavy communications cables were being laid back to army headquarters and photographers and war correspondents arrived, milling around among the ever-increasing staff. Todd and Van Fleet were busy conferring with two- and three-star generals. Clearly, something unusual was going on.

The rain of the previous day had given way to a cloud-free beautiful summer day. When everyone had arrived, the Division Commander—General Barton—began the briefing.

"Today," he said, pointing to a map on the wall, "is the day our forces will break out from the Normandy peninsula into the French countryside on our way to Paris. In about an hour, some 1600 heavy bombers will begin bombing the German lines. They will fly in formation of 15 planes. After they have passed, which will take about four hours, the Third Army—under the command of General Patton—will move with its tank divisions through our present lines and advance toward Paris. Two Infantry Divisions— the 4th and the 9th—will follow the tanks.

"Half an hour from now, fighter bombers will put down colored flares along the road you see on this map, roughly seven kilometers behind the front, in the German-held area. That will be the bomb line. The first bombs will be dropped at that line, then the subsequent bombers will release their loads moving toward us and will stop at the St. Lo-Coutances road about two kilometers from where we are now.

"That is where the bombing mission will end and Patton's mission begins. The idea is to trap the German units and to prevent them from leaving the attack area too easily. From this hill, you'll be able to observe the whole action. It will be quite a spectacle."

There was great excitement in the room. Field phones were ringing, questions were asked and answered, and the anticipation of this historic event about to unfold created a nervous energy. Many of us, me included, had gone outside, to get a better view of the terrain and to look at the sky for the oncoming air armada. Suddenly, we heard screeching followed by a huge explosion. We rushed into the command post to hear that a stray German anti-tank shell had hit the house sideways, pierced one wall and exited the other wall, and then exploded harmlessly in the field behind us. There was rubble and dust everywhere but miraculously no one was hurt.

Newspaper and cameramen had been invited to observe and report. With notebooks in hand and cameras flashing, they inter- viewed everyone. We all were happy to talk with them. It was at that time that I met Ernie Pile. Most of us had gone outside when the action began. We saw our fighter planes in the far distance marking the bomb line with red, blue, and yellow smoke bombs. Shortly after that, we heard the droning sound of the first B-25s flying in. High up in the sky, they looked like bees about half an inch long, flying in formation of 15. German anti-aircraft fire went up, we could see the red tracer bullets and the white puffs of exploding shells in the sky. As time went on, a few planes were hit and tumbled down through the sky.

After the first few hundred or so bombers had flown by, we noticed that something was terribly wrong. They were bombing much closer to us than they should have been and as the next planes flew by, they continued to drop their bombs ever closer to our lines. It became evident that soon they would hit our own positions and that included our command post.

Then we realized what was happening. A slight wind had blown the smoke of the bomb line flares in our direction and the pilots of the first group, seeing only the smoke, not the muddied small road, started bombing about two miles closer to us than planned. There was no way of communicating with the B-25s. They were either out of range or were observing radio silence. We knew now that we were in the line of bombing but could do nothing about it. There was no panic—just a feeling of absolute doom. The excited chatter of the morning quieted down until eventually no one spoke. It was now just a matter of time.

Everyone looked up at the sky. Silence. I was in the courtyard and could see the planes dropping their bombs ever closer to us. Then we could hear the explosions. Finally, they were directly overhead.

Falling bombs sound like a train coming at you. At that point, in panic I ran into the closest barn and hid under a wooden hay cart. Next to me lay Ernie Pile. I recall that we commented about the absurdity of our situation and the feeling of total helplessness. The bombing lasted only a few minutes. Then we heard explosions some distance behind us and realized we had survived.

Once again I had been extremely lucky. There were numerous bomb craters around us, but the Command Post had not been hit at all. Our Division—we soon learned—had suffered relatively light casualties. The 9th Division, to our right, was hit much more severely. Their commander, General McNair, and most of his staff had been killed and the Division had been so decimated that it could not participate in the breakthrough.

Ernie Pyle had talked with me earlier. Now that we were out of danger, he asked me what I planned to do after the war. My hope had been to work for a newspaper and Pyle graciously volunteered to write me a letter of commendation right there and then.

It was addressed to Manchester Boddy, Managing Editor of the Los Angeles Daily News. He gave it to me and I sent it to Albertine for safekeeping. The letter survived the censors—though a number of references identifying our location on that eventful day had been neatly cut out. I still have the letter. I never used it. As the war in Europe was coming to an end, Ernie Pyle had gone to the Pacific Theater. Reporting on the invasion of one of the small Japanese-occupied islands, he was killed. Back in LA after the war, it just didn't feel right to use the letter of a dead man. It is one of the few souvenirs that I have of WWII.

The other notable person I met that day was Ernest Hemingway. He heard of my job and was intrigued by the idea of meeting newly captured prisoners. He asked if I would mind if he joined my unit for a few days. Of course, I was flattered and excited but, alas, I was far too immature to fully appreciate the great opportunity this presented.

I was aware of Hemingway's fame, had read many of his books and short stories and so was very much awed by his presence. But I did not want to admit this—certainly not to him. I did not want to be perceived as a "star-struck little boy". So I played it cool and never inquired of his writing or his experiences. For the two weeks he was with me, we spoke only of the events at hand, the war and the prisoners. One day he met my friend David Brooks who talked with him of his job as leader of the I&R platoon (Intelligence and Reconnaissance). Immediately Hemingway decided to participate in one of their missions. When he came back, he told everybody that he had manned the 50-caliber machine gun but, unfortunately, they had not encountered any enemy. Of course, every one in the regiment heard the story.

A few days later Mr. Hemingway was ordered to leave the front because he had violated the Geneva Convention. As a war correspondent, he was forbidden to carry arms and to engage the enemy. I felt quite bad that he was gone, punished for such a minor offence.

After what we called "The Breakthrough", the Allied offensive, led by Patton's Third Army was so successful that we started to speculate how soon we would be in Paris. Hemingway and I made a $10 bet as to when we would capture the city. Now he was gone and out of my life.

After we had broken out of Normandy, all our moves forward were by jeep. Early on, we had lowered the windshields, which were constantly covered with dust. Now we were alerted that the retreating Germans had strung piano wires across many roads and that a number of jeep drivers had been severely injured. One of my men, Alex, was a wonderful handy man. From somewhere, he "liberated" a welding torch, found a few iron rods, which he then welded, vertically onto the center of the front bumper of the jeeps. Although we never encountered any piano wires, it made us feel much safer. Soon most vehicles had similar contraptions.

27

Even though our tank units were engaging the enemy well ahead of us, there was still a lot of fighting on the way to Paris. I was usually about a kilometer from the front so that prisoners could be interrogated almost immediately after capture. At that distance, we were mostly exposed to artillery and mortar fire—always dangerous, but rarely deadly.

We passed the Falaise Gap where the tank battle—now famous—had just taken place. For about 15 kilometers, on both sides of a country road, we passed burned out tanks, many still smoldering, mostly Germans, but a good number of ours as well. Here, in one of the most famous battles of the war, the Germans had lost their main tank force west of Paris. Once again, our victory was assured by our complete command of the air. Our Air Force fighters, almost unopposed, severely punished the German tank force. Had Hitler been able to spare more of his fighter planes from the Eastern Front, the battle of Falaise would have been much more difficult to win.

Every day now the front moved forward and so did my unit. Though it was clearly a sign of success, I hated to move. It meant leaving a relatively safe place where I had just survived and moving to a new place fraught with unknown dangers. Usually I tried to find a farmhouse or a barn or even a cave to quarter my men but this one evening there was nothing around, just empty fields. Even Todd had found no shelter fort for the CP, so the only choice was to start digging foxholes. Just as I was deciding whether it was worth the effort, "Bed Time Charlie," the lone German plane, which flew over our position almost every evening, decided to drop his load of bombs directly on us.

One of my men had just started to dig. He took cover in the shallow foxhole and I jumped in on top of him and immediately felt the concussion and thunder of exploding bombs. Shrapnel, earth and rocks hit my lower body. The whole thing was over in a few seconds. I knew I had been hit but I was able to get up. I was covered with rocks and dirt but to my great surprise, I had no wounds, no hurt except the concussion in my ears. I looked around me, I knew a bomb had exploded nearby but there was no evidence of anything. No crater, nothing.

We had not yet laid any phone lines so I decided to walk over to the regimental CP to see what had happened to them. To get there I had to leave the field we were in, climb down to a road beneath my field and the adjacent one. The road ran parallel to our encampment but about 10 feet lower. A jeep was there, destroyed in the middle of a huge bomb crater—the driver and three men killed—two feet from where I had been, just 10 feet below. All the bomb shrapnel had hit the embankment. Had the bomb hit just a yard on the other side of me, in the field rather than in the road, I would have bee killed instantly. The CP—by the way—was intact.

A few weeks after Falaise, we began to pass road signs: Paris 125 km, then Paris 83 km, and soon we reached the outskirts of the capital. The advance now was relatively easy; we met with very little resistance. Clearly, the Germans had decided to cede the area this side of Paris to us. With them in retreat, there were few prisoners to interrogate. Instead I made contact with the French Resistance—here called the FFI. (In the south of France the anti-German resistance was called the "Maquis") They gave us extremely valuable information, primarily about German troop movements. Most of them were young people from local villages, who now proudly wore their homemade FFI armbands openly.

We were steadily approaching Paris but as we reached the outskirts of the capital, we were ordered to halt. There still was no serious German resistance so the sudden stop made no sense. By the second day of waiting, we heard the reason for the delay. SHAEF (Supreme Headquarter Allied Expeditionary Force) and specifically General Eisenhower had been persuaded by General De Gaulle that Paris should be liberated by French troops.

The 2nd French Armored Division, coming from Algeria was given that honor. They were now on their way to Paris and would reach the capital in a few days. Meanwhile all Allied Forces outside Paris were to wait for the French to capture their own capital.

That afternoon Major Todd came over and said: "Looks like we're going to sit here for a few more days. Do you know Paris?"

"Oh yes," I lied.

"Well then," said Todd, "let's take a jeep and have a look at the city, Ok?"

So Major Todd, Sergeant Sternberg, my driver Johnny Baer, and I loaded up and, thus, we were the first Americans—although unofficially—to enter Paris. The sun was just setting as we drove into town. Immediately, we were surrounded by a jubilant crowd of Parisians, who were well aware that for them the war was about to end. They were milling around in the streets celebrating the first wisps of freedom. They knew an American jeep when they saw one and long before we arrived downtown, the crowd insisted we stop at a bar.

After many toasts and songs, one guy insisted he wanted to show us Place Pigalle. He pushed his fellow celebrant aside, got into our jeep and we took off for the famous red-light district. By now it was dark, Paris was still under strict blackout. Thus we arrived at Pigalle without being noticed. Our first stop was another bistro. Again we were feted with drinks and cheers, then we moved on to a stately four-story house. Our guide knocked on the door and yelled: "Babette, open up, I brought you a bunch of Americans!"

Babette turned out to be a charming madame, her girls beautiful and both exciting and excited. That night, Paris captured us. The girl I selected—or who was assigned to me, (who knows?) was very sweet and very young. She was pleased that I spoke French and asked many questions about the war but happily our conversations were spiced, by frequent amorous interruptions. She insisted that she hated Germans, slept only with French soldiers. Actually I was quite taken by her and remembered her name—Josie.

The night was short, interrupted by a brief air raid (German?). No one seemed to care and very early in the morning, our guide came to take us back to the spot where we had entered Paris. Back at our unit—smug and happy—we kept our mouths shut.

The 2nd Armored Division (French) finally arrived and officially took Paris, though not very efficiently. Many of the men were native Parisians, who had been separated from their families for many years. Now they simply drove their tanks home. One can hardly blame them but they left the town in quite a mess. There was still a German rearguard in downtown and no one to fight them. So the next day, we were ordered to move in and, thus, I entered Paris a second time.

By then General de Gaulle had arrived, and the following day to the jubilant acclaim of what seemed to be the whole population of Paris, the 2nd Armored Division paraded down the Champs Elysees. This was followed by a ceremony in the Cite where de Gaulle—after a very long speech—was presented with the key to the city. I was among the huge crowd when suddenly shots were fired from the rooftops nearby. Everyone scattered in panic but soon order was restored and the ceremony continued. Spasmodic small firefights continued for a few more days, primarily in downtown Paris. Evidently, a group of die-hard Nazis was hoping to recapture Paris and the rest of France. They did not succeed.

28

After Paris, we continued our advance toward Germany. I was promoted to First Lieutenant, then to Captain, and upon the recommendation of Major Todd, was awarded the Bronze Star. Sergeant Sternberg became Lieutenant Sternberg, Johnny Baer became Sergeant Baer, and Alex continued to fix everything that needed fixing.

By autumn, the Front was in the Ardennes, and my regiment was involved in the battle of the Hürtgen Forest. At the far end of the forest, the Germans had put up a formidable defense line supported by tanks and artillery. There we were—stopped, surrounded by the dense forests. Every attempt to break out resulted in heavy casualties but no progress. It was fall, raining and cold. Trapped amidst the trees, we were exposed to continuous artillery fire.

The Germans were using airburst shells. They exploded not when they hit the ground but rather when they came in contact with the tree branches. Consequently, we experienced a constant shower of shrapnel. The dense tree roots made digging foxholes virtually impossible. We were stuck for about 12 days—cold, wet, sleepless and frightened. There were no prisoners to interrogate.

My sole job was to find ways for me and my men to survive. There was not much to do. We tried to use the jeeps for shelter by lying under the vehicle but the wet ground made this so uncomfortable that we soon gave up. Alex eventually built a shelter from fallen branches. We all huddled inside this very leaky tent and although it was obviously no protection from the shrapnel, it provided a psychological "safe- house". As usual I was within a few hundred yards of the regimental CP, about a half-mile from the Front where conditions must have really been terrible.

Finally, after many unsuccessful attempts, we were able to break the deadlock and force a German retreat. Weakened from the considerable casualties, our Division was replaced and moved to a relatively quiet sector of the front, near a small river. The Germans on the other side of the river were either too weak to attempt a crossing or they may have even retreated beyond it. In any case, there was no action and it gave us a chance to recuperate.

The oldest man on my team was Sergeant Corcoran. A happy-go-lucky 26-year-old Irish fellow whose German grandmother had insisted that he become bi-lingual, Jim spoke fluent German but with a rather strange accent. Among us, he was the only married man. Usually orders for special missions came by phone.

Major Todd would call for a jeep and three men to go on a patrol in a given area, either to capture some prisoners or to see what kind of fire we might draw. These missions sounded more dangerous than they actually were because as soon as we took any mortar, artillery or machine gun fire, we would hightail it out of the area. The first shells rarely hit close to their target. The more comprehensive missions of this kind were assigned to the I&R platoon.

As far as prisoners were concerned, we left that to soldiers on the frontline. Except for my Normandy adventure we never captured anyone! Invariably, every time I got an order from Todd, Jim Corcoran would come to me, smiling sadly and with his heavy Irish brogue say: "Captain, did I ever show you the pictures of my wife and child?" It was rare for any soldier ever to address another soldier by rank. Of course, I had seen Jim's photos many times. It was Jim's joke and it always worked. I never assigned him to a Special Mission.

One evening, while we were camped near a rather quiet front by the river, Jim asked for permission to take a jeep and trailer.

"Why," I asked. "Secret mission," he smiled. "I just need it for this night."

Next morning, he proudly took me to the jeep. Both the vehicle and the trailer were filled with wooden crates. Each crate contained 48 bottles of Martel, one of the finest French cognacs.

"My God, Jim, how did you do that?"

On the map he showed me a little village about three miles across the river in German held territory. From a front line soldier, Jim had heard that there was a warehouse nearby with all that booze. Daily patrols had established that the Germans were on the other side of the warehouse, so Jim decided that night to take a shot at it, to drive deep into German lines in order to capture his booty. Fantastic! But now we had a problem. How were we going to transport 20 cases of liquor? At best we had room for only three or four. Our jeeps were full with equipment and ammunition.

I took my problem along with a bottle to Todd. Very quickly, we struck a deal. For the payment of five cases, he would transport our stuff, and we could have access to it any time we wanted. From that day on, we drank brandy for the rest of the war.

29

It was now early November. Since the Division was still waiting for replacements from the Hürtgen Forest losses, I got permission for a five-day leave and chose to go to Paris. This time I was a tourist and began to really see the town. While walking along the Tuileries, approaching the Place de la Concorde, it occurred to me that Hemingway might well be in Paris. If he were there, undoubtedly, he would be at the Hôtel de Crillon, the finest hotel in Paris. I walked over to the main bar of the hotel and asked the bartender if Mr. Hemingway happened to be around.

"Oh," he replied, "he doesn't come in until about 7 o'clock."

It was not long to wait and, sure enough, about 7:30, in walked Hemingway. We had a cordial reunion. We sat at the bar. He bought me a drink and although it had only been a few months since he had left my Unit, we had a lot to talk about. That was when I remembered the bet we had made about when Paris would be freed.

"You know," I said, "I won that bet! You owe me $10."

Hemingway laughed. "You're right," he said and took out his wallet. He found a $10 bill, took his pen and on the edge of the bill, he wrote: "To my friend Walter Bodlander with sincere admiration, Ernest Hemingway."

He handed it to me and with a smile said: "Now, we're even."

I took the bill and looked at it. Here I was—this very sophisticated adult, not star struck, not impressed at all by fame, and so I had to prove it in case anyone had any doubts about it.

So I took the bill, smiled, and said: "Thanks, and now I will buy you a drink. With that, I called the bartender for a refill for both of us and paid him with the $10 bill I had just "earned".

Hemingway was not amused. He fell quiet for a moment, did not wait for his drink and said: "Well, I have to go now, so long."

I never heard from him again. This was one of the most childish and tactless—and I might add—stupidest things I had ever done in my life.

One night, toward the end of my leave, I found myself in the Pigalle area. It was late and I was ready to take the subway back to my hotel. The station was deserted. I did not know that metro service halted at 11 p.m. during the war. Now it was way past midnight. The streets were empty and dark. Paris was still under black out. With no taxi in sight, I started walking back to my hotel.

Across the street I heard footsteps going in the same direction. I noticed it was a soldier and went over to talk to him. Turned out he was an Aussie, caught like me without transportation. As we walked in the dark, I told him of my escapade the day before liberation. It was in this very area that I had ended up in a bordello, I told him. Just then we came to a three-story stately apartment building, which seemed vaguely familiar. Of course, in the blackout I wasn't certain but we began to laugh and decided we had nothing to lose.

So we began to knock on the wooden nine-foot door. No answer. We were about to move on when a female voice yelled from one of the windows: "What the hell do you want, we're closed. It's too late.

I yelled back: "Madame, I'm one of the American soldiers who was here the day before…" I didn't get the chance to finish the sentence.

"Oh, mon Dieu," she screamed. "Just a minute."

Seconds later she opened the door and embraced me. Then she yelled for Josie: "Your American friend is here." Josie arrived, at first a bit petulant, then when she recognized me, she was delighted. My Aussie friend had already moved upstairs with a "petite fille" in tow. Madame brought out some of her finest liquors and after a toast she ordered us off to bed.

I really liked Josie but something did not click. I felt she had just finished with a "client." She, on the other hand, was annoyed that I was not eager to jump into bed. I had already undressed and was sitting at the edge of the bed when our talk became an argument. Now Josie got furious and started yelling at me: "You ass hole, you bastard, you no-good..." including some French words that I didn't understand but whose meanings were quite clear. Then, in a final fit of anger, she jumped out of bed, grabbed my uniform and threw it out the window.

This struck us both as so funny that we began to laugh and, thus, the night ended in peaceful embrace. Luckily, the window led to the courtyard, not to the street. Next morning Josie insisted I go naked to retrieve my clothes. This was the last day of my leave. I promised her I'd be back but we both knew this was the end of a strange little affair.

30

Shortly after my Paris leave, we were encamped behind the lines as a reserve unit. It was the beginning of winter and we were in a mountainous area, which we had just captured from the Germans. We found a group of bombed-out bunkers—cold, humid and dark—but the structures offered shelter from rain, snow flurries and artillery, and so they became our refuge.

We were supposed to rest but in the windy wet misery, it seemed more punishment then reward. It was here that for the first time, we saw a new German weapon—the buzz bomb. This was the much-touted secret weapon, which Hitler had announced. It was called the V1 (Vergeltungswaffen—Retaliation Weapon) and would, according to Nazi propaganda, turn the fortunes of war in favor of Germany. This V-1 was literally a flying bomb. With a wing-span of about 12 to 15 feet, it flew at relatively low speed and altitude right over our lines, propelled by a motor that made the put-put sound which gave it the name "Buzz Bomb".

The V-1 were destined for London and as they flew by, we tried to shoot them down. For miles, you could see our red tracer bullets in the sky. These slow, low flying bombs were an easy target, we certainly hit many but they seemed impervious to our 50-caliber machine gun fire and they flew right on. About 30 of them would fly over on a daily basis what we called the Buzz

Bomb Alley. Occasionally, a bomb's engine would be hit. Then the put-put noise suddenly ceased, and the bomb would begin to glide silently, losing both speed and altitude, and then drop aimlessly with an enormous explosion. One of these disabled bombs dropped short of its target near our headquarters, miles behind the front. It killed a number of our men.

I later learned that among the casualties was the very officer who earlier, while we had been on maneuvers in the U.S., had suggested that I should apply for Military Intelligence as he had done, since the job, he said, would be way behind the front and much less dangerous than Field Artillery. His death was a sad irony!

The V-1s did not last very long. They were not effective and rarely hit their target. Soon the Germans had developed the much more lethal V-2. This was an actual missile—probably the first high altitude missile ever used in warfare. It, too, was aimed at London and other major British cities and was extremely powerful. A single V-2 could destroy an entire city block, thus the name "Blockbuster".

I never saw one. They flew much too high to be seen and when they hit, there was no warning whatsoever. For months the English population had to live with the possibility that at any moment one of these rockets would hit them. The danger ended only when Allied forces captured the launching sites in Germany.

Just before Christmas we were moved towards the front again. This time to Luxembourg. We were still in reserve, and basically inactive. I heard that a prominent Luxembourg family living in a nearby chateau was giving a "Thank-you" party for any American soldier who could attend. Major Todd did not object, so I took Johnny Baer and my jeep. We drove the 30 kilometers to the castle where we were greeted with open arms.

In the huge ancient dining hall, an enormous table had been set for 20 or more people and for hours wonderful food and wines were served. As more soldiers arrived throughout the evening, those of us who had already gorged ourselves made room for the newcomers. A string trio (or was it a quartet?) played Christmas music and after the food, cigarettes and cigars were served. Our host and hostess, recently liberated, showered us not only with food and drink but also with a number of handmade gifts. There were "V" for victory pins made from silver coins, napkins with an embroidered flag of Luxembourg and other such memorabilia.

The room was full of soldiers, at least 30 or so; the mood—festive and happy. As the wine flowed, we began to sing along with the violins. As the evening progressed, I soon went through my stages of intoxication: happiness, drowsiness, exhaustion, and sleep.

I remember being awakened literally lying under the banquet table. It was early the next morning and someone shook me into consciousness. With extreme urgency, I was told to report to my unit at once. Word had just come that the Germans had launched an offensive and that the Allied lines had been broken. So Johnny and I drove back to our Unit but we did not get very far.

An American outpost stopped us at gunpoint. They wanted to know where we had come from and where we were going. In short they were skeptical about our identity. We were completely baffled. Then they informed us they had information that the German army was using captured American equipment and uniforms to infiltrate our lines.

The situation became very ugly as soon as I opened my mouth. My heavy German accent was a clear give-away. With his revolver pointed at me, the lieutenant in charge asked me where I lived in the U.S. I replied: "Los Angeles". Then my bad luck turned worse since one of his men knew the town. They asked me to describe Glendale in relation to Hollywood. Of course, I couldn't do it since I had been in the States less than nine months and knew very little about Los Angeles. They asked Johnny some questions about baseball, which he, too, could not answer. We were ordered out of the jeep for further questioning.

Now their rifles were pointed at us. I tried to argue that if we were, indeed, German infiltrators, I would have used my fully loaded 50-caliber machinegun on my jeep when they had stopped me. The lieutenant was not completely convinced but we came to a compromise. I would surrender the jeep, the machine gun, and our handguns. Two of his men would drive us back to my Unit. When we arrived, captured by our own forces, Todd thought this was the funniest thing ever. The Regiment staff could not get over it and I got ribbed for weeks.

This was the beginning of the Battle of the Bulge, which lasted for more than a month. American casualties were very heavy—more than 19,000 killed, 47,000 wounded and 23,000 taken as prisoners. My very good friend in later life, Arthur Rubenstein, was among those taken prisoner.

The German forces almost succeeded in their attempt to push us into the sea. They were stopped by the heroic resistance of our forces holding Bastogne. The famous response: "Nuts" by the American commander to the German request for surrender is well known to all interested in WWII history.

My unit was not involved in the fierce fighting. We were ordered to hold a sector recently recaptured from the Germans. Our Air Force was heavily involved in assisting the ground forces. We were very close to the front and often were bombed and strafed by our own planes.

Friendly fire casualties took place frequently and were an enormous problem. Finally, a solution was found. We were issued large plastic panels, rolled up like carpets—four red and four yellow. Every day we would unfold them and lay them out on the field according to a specific daily code. One red, two yellow, for example, would tell our pilots that we were friendly troops. It helped a lot.

From a military point of view, that January and February were uneventful; but from a personal view, they were miserable. We lived again in bombed-out German bunkers—cold, wet and dirty. The dangerous frontline situation demanded that only ammunition and weapons were transported forward. Consequently, we received no hot food and had to live on K-rations. At night the temperature went down to -15 degrees (Celsius). Daytime was not much better. Snow and sleet kept us wet. Most of us stopped shaving, and sanitation was minimum. Almost everyone had lice. Since we were not involved in any fighting, there were no prisoners to interrogate. War became a dreary routine of fear, misery and inaction. The only diversion was trying to shoot down the buzz bombs, which kept flying overhead.

31

Then everything changed. Orders came that we were to participate in a special task force consisting of tanks, armored cars and motorized infantry. The mission: a forced push to the Rhine in order to capture any bridge still intact. Speed was of the essence. The unit was not to be engaged in fighting except when necessary to move on. Four other task forces were moving on parallel roads down the mountains with the same objective. It was a race to determine which unit would get to a usable bridge first.

More than half a century has passed since that day. Though the mist of time has dimmed many memories, the feelings I experienced at that moment are as vivid today as they were on that cold wet night in the Ardennes. Until then we had fought the Germans in France.

Now finally, and for the first time, I would be involved in the conquest of Germany itself. I wondered what the German population would think and feel as we drove through their villages. I did not feel anger or hatred, just an enormous elation—an overwhelming awareness of successful revenge. This was IT. This had been my reason for being involved in this war. For the first time since the landing, I was genuinely happy. I had returned to Germany, a conqueror.

Our advance began in the dark hours of 4 a.m. with the distant roar of our tanks warming up. Then the noise intensified as tank after tank passed us, then armored cars fell in line, then we were waved in and behind us came more armored infantry. Thus, this huge line-up moved slowly in total blackout along a narrow dirt road downhill from the mountains toward the Rhine—some 100 kilometers ahead. The drive was slow, not more than 10 miles per hour and basically uneventful. The convoy stopped frequently, then would move on again. We had no idea what was going on at the head of the column and though we would occasionally pass a disabled German army vehicle, I never heard a shot fired.

As daylight broke, we passed the first German village. Farmers were standing by their barns, people stood outside their houses—silent, stunned and probably incredulous. As the day moved on, we passed through more villages. Some larger ones had German army units stationed there.

The situation was always the same. Civilians and soldiers stood silently and obviously in awe as we passed by. There was absolutely no resistance. Clearly, they were completely surprised and unable to engage our very superior force. So they just stood there as we rolled by and we, too, did not engage them but just, as ordered, moved on.

We drove for well over 14 hours, and the only casualty was an occasional armored car or even a tank whose driver had fallen asleep and wound up in a ditch. Then we were stopped again, this time for at least an hour. We had no idea what was happening. Eventually came the word: Another task force had beaten us to the Rhine and had captured a bridge at Remagen.

It was disappointing that we were not the first to accomplish the objective but the fact that U.S. forces had reached the Rhine was exhilarating. No one had been sure that a usable bridge could be found. The Rhine is a large fast flowing river, a major obstacle to our advancing army. The capture of the undamaged and usable Remagen Bridge made the crossing of the Rhine much easier and was a major reason for the rapid deterioration of the German resistance.

Many years later, in the late 1970s, while traveling in Europe, I wanted to show my wife Carol the famous bridge at Remagen.

for headquarters and I had billeted my men in a two-story hotel, opposite the church and its yard.

That night, for the first time since the Normandy invasion, I had taken off my boots and gone to sleep in a bed. Gunshots and flames awakened me. From my second story window, I saw that most of our vehicles we had parked in the churchyard were on fire. In the street below, a group of German soldiers were marching, jubilantly noisy through the town, shooting wildly at the buildings.

Clearly, they had entered the town, overwhelmed our guards and were now ready to recapture Oxenfurt. I tried to put on my boots but could not find them in the dark. The only light available was the flickering of the burning cars. Johnny Baer and Lt. Sternberg were with me, the rest of my men were on the first floor. The field phone rang. The terrified operator asked what to do. He could not get through to the command post. I told him to arm himself as best he could and to stay put.

No one was prepared for this counterattack and very few of us had any weapons at hand. All I had was my pistol. Some hand grenades were in the jeep, now burning. Downstairs, the men had two rifles. I was certain that soon we would be killed or captured and all we could do was to wait.

Somehow the Germans must have decided they were not strong enough to enter the buildings. After about three hours of roaming through town, they left defiantly singing the Nazi Horst Wessel hymn. I am sorry to say that although four of our guards were killed and two wounded, the Germans suffered no casualties and we never learned which daredevil unit had attacked us.

As we moved south through forests we saw hundreds of Nazi fighter planes parked along the roads. They were well camouflaged and had escaped detection by our Air Force. They were intact but useless to the Germans since the country literally was out of gas. The presence of these planes gave some credence to the rumors that the Nazis planned to organize a resistance movement in the South, the fierce "Werewolf Redoubt" housed in the German Alps. I had heard and reported these stories, but there was never any concrete evidence pointing to a Werewolf organization. Events proved that all this was—at best—hopeful thinking by some German die-hards. The Nazi hierarchy had disintegrated so fast that there was no fight left in them and the population at large, now fully aware that the war was lost, was in no mood to resist. In fact, by now numerous civilian "volunteers" were trying to help us. Pointing south they would say: "Wehrmacht dahin" (there).

32

This was about the time when my driver Johnny and I were driving towards an adjacent village hoping to make contact with one of our sister units also advancing towards Munich. We were on an unpaved country road moving leisurely when Johnny jumped out of the jeep without bothering to stop it and drove it into a ditch.

"There's someone in the woods," Johnny whispered. "I heard something."

We had been driving so slowly that no one was hurt. I turned the jeep engine off, all was quiet.

"You're nuts," I said. "Let's get the jeep back on the road."

Just then I, too, heard some rustling. Armed with our rifles, we headed for the woods. Not very far. Out of the undergrowth—hands raised high, emerged a rather tattered German soldier, an officer. On second glance, we realized he was a General. He was unarmed, alone and eager to surrender. He told me that he had lost contact with his staff when our tank units had routed his division in a short but decisive firefight.

He had been walking along the main roads hoping to surrender but all he had seen were endless columns of American tanks and armored vehicles. So he decided to wait a day or two until things settled down a bit. When he heard our jeep, he decided to come out but we had been driving too fast. When we had our little accident, he was ready to turn himself in. We searched him for weapons, took his wristwatch and a pocketknife, and then drove him back to our unit. He sat in the back of the jeep and, occasionally, I looked back at him. What fascinated me was a gold and red scarf he was wearing. Throughout the war all of us suffered from burned and inflamed necks. In summer it was the sun; in winter, the wet wool of dirty, sweaty shirts rubbing against the skin caused painful inflammations.

In Normandy we had used silk from abandoned parachutes as scarves but as time passed they got lost. Later on, there were no more parachutes and I often looked for something to replace the lost silk. Now here was a perfect opportunity to get a decent scarf for my aching neck. I toyed with the idea of taking it but reluctantly decided against it. Though it was certainly not part of his uniform, it was also not dangerous to us and, thus, was not "allowed" to be confiscated. Without further ado, we delivered our prisoner—scarf and all—to the appropriate authorities.

Munich was captured a few days later shortly before the end of the war. Like all major cities, Munich had been bombed incessantly, but as we entered the inner city many buildings were still standing. On closer look however you could see that they were mostly empty shells. The outer walls stood but inside, the buildings had been burned out. People lived in cellars. Water, food and electricity were either not available or—at best—in very short supply.

The 8th infantry regiment's headquarters was set up in the suburb of Gauting. I was to billet my men in any available house and soon found a very comfortable villa, un-bombed and unoccupied—quite intact. It was a pleasant two-story house, well furnished and clean when we moved in. The photos on the wall and coffee table showed a smiling SS officer and his family. Thus, no one cared that the place became more and more abused as time went on. I stayed there for about two months, then I got a new assignment. More about that later.

Well supplied with food, cigarettes and candy bars and with no duty to perform, this was a time of rest and play. German girls were plentiful and they flocked to us as if attracted by magnets. Booze of all kinds liberated from abandoned cellars and my unexhaustable supply of Martel fueled never-ending parties.

The girls pretended to be apolitical, their only motive survival. They all told us how terrible the last months had been, how the constant bombings had taken their toll. There was a saying, they said: "Everything is getting worse. Only one thing is getting better: the morals are getting worse."

All of them had lost homes or contact with their families, and every one hated the war but most of all, they hated the Nazis. The latter was a universal theme. I had little cause and no particular interest to associate with the population at large, but there were occasional interactions and inevitably conversations began or ended with the assertion: "Understand that I hated the Nazis." Indeed, for the eight months that I spent in Germany after the war, I encountered no Nazis. They were all somewhere else.

33

About that time I heard that the U.S. State Department had opened its first office in Salzburg, Austria, and it occurred to me that working in Europe for a better world would be logical employment for me. So I contacted the head of the embassy, a Mr. Denby, gave him a short resume, and asked if I could come to see him. He agreed and after our meeting, following his suggestion, I applied for a transfer from the U.S. Army to the U.S. State Department.

Mr. Denby had offered me a transfer "in rank", meaning in the State Department I would have similar status as a captain and get the same pay as I had had in the Army. The application went all the way to Eisenhower's headquarters, was approved and then went to the State Department in Washington D.C. where it was disapproved. Reason: The applicant was not an American-born citizen and, thus, could not work as a career State Department employee.

It was suggested I could work as "a temp" with no professional standing. I declined. All this had taken well over three months. The rejection was very disappointing and somewhat insulting but soon I would realize that the bigoted (and anti-Semitic) State Department had done me a great favor.

The Truman idea of the post-World War II world was very different from the one Roosevelt (and I) had anticipated. The idea to contain the Soviet Union rather than to co-operate with them led rapidly to the Cold War, and at no time was there a guarantee that "cold" would not deteriorate into "hot". Thus, the policies enacted by the State Department were not what I would have wanted to work for. I'm certain that I would not have lasted long in the job.

As the war ended, combat veterans were allowed to apply for discharge from the service. A point system had been devised. Points were given for length of service and special additional points if one had participated in what was designated as a "battle". Since I was considered a Frontline veteran, I had plenty of points and could have been discharged almost immediately.

But I was waiting for word from the State Department, so I opted to stay in Germany. There was now no more need for tactical intelligence. Consequently, my team was detached from the 4th Division and assigned to Counter-Intelligence. The new job: assisting in demobilizing German Army units and finding and arresting war criminals. Counter-Intelligence had issued a list of specific persons to be apprehended in addition to what was called the Automatic Arrest Category. The latter was defined as any officer of the armed forces above the rank of Colonel and all SS personnel. However, before I could begin my new duties, I was given a special assignment.

The German 10th Army had been involved in bitter fighting with the British 8th Army in Italy and several German Divisions had asked permission to surrender to U.S. forces in Munich rather than to the British in Milan. They feared retaliation from the forces they had faced so recently. Permission was granted and the task fell to me to take care of the surrender.

A football field next to an abandoned high school and an adjacent bombed-out city block, which had since been vacated and cleared, became a temporary tent city ready to house about 10,000 men. We were provided with 40 typewriters (but no typists), a delousing station, one company of MP guards and a field kitchen. I was assured that I could get additional help if needed from the newly installed Military Government. So about in the middle of May, two fully armed German Divisions with 9,000 men including tanks and armored cars rolled into Munich—a force vastly superior to the few American units in town—and they formally surrendered to me. For good measure, about 1,000 prisoners of war who had surrendered to us were added to the group.

The basic task was to list every soldier and to indicate his disposition. Anyone below the rank of major and whose home was in Western Germany or who had connection to a family farm was to be released immediately. All higher ranking officers and all SS men of any rank were to remain prisoners. Soldiers whose homes were not in Western Germany were to be sent to a special holding prison area to be released at a later date.

I asked for the 10 highest ranking German officers to report to me and ordered them to oversee the following procedures. All weapons and vehicles were to be parked in a designated area. The men were to be divided into groups of 200 each, classified A1, B1, etc. After A1 would come A2, B2... Each man had to know to which group he belonged. Every group had to have a Commander whose name was to be given to me. The groups were given tent areas and were not to move from there. Each of the 10 ranking officers was in charge of 50 groups. They would be told when their groups were to line up for food, delousing, or interrogation for disposition. The highest-ranking officer among the 10 was to report to me daily or whenever there was any emergency.

Again, I was amazed at the cooperation and the discipline. The surrender had begun in the morning, by nightfall all men were housed, either in tents or sleeping bags. I had eight men in my team, all fluent in German. We had set up the typewriter banks in the gym of the high school, and each day prisoners lined up for interrogation and disposition in groups of 200. German soldiers manned the typewriters, listing every man's name, rank, home and final disposition. But first, of course, they had to pass interrogation by my men.

We always asked members of SS units to step forward and some did. They and the higher army officers were immediately registered and sent back to their tents. The remaining men were briefly interrogated. First, they all had to undress to the waist and raise their arms. The SS had tattooed their members under the arm with their blood type, so it was quite easy to identify the SS men. Some, however, had anticipated that the tattoos would identify them and had tried to remove the telltale tattoos, usually by attempting to burn them off with a lighted cigarette. So anyone with a scar under the arm was assumed to be an SS soldier and taken out of the line-up.

Then came the questions of their home. Of course, the story spread very fast that anyone from Southern Germany or with a farm connection would be released and so the stock answer always was: "I'm from a little village here in Bavaria and my family has a small farm." If they were not SS, we didn't care; we gave them a travel pass. They were free to leave immediately.

Every evening, the ranking general reported to me on the progress of the operation. That officer happened to be the very general who had surrendered to me a bit earlier and, of course, we recognized each other. His reports were brief, to the point, and our meeting totally impersonal. Then one evening, he requested permission to ask me a personal question: How is it that I spoke such fluent German. I told him a bit of my background and that began a continuing conversation.

Every evening after his daily report, he asked permission to sit down and then we would talk about the war, politics and life. The General was probably in his late 40s, well educated and very well brought up. The tone of our meetings was always mutually respectful. Often I was surprised how little hate or anger I felt on these evenings.

Somehow this man did not seem to represent the horrible disgusting Nazi philosophy but when he began to tell me his story, I started to get a glimpse of the duality of these people: cultured and bright while—at the same time—cold and ruthless. It was a chilling, sad experience for me. A career officer, the General was apolitical until Hitler's astounding successes in foreign affairs between 1935 and 1938. He mentioned the main ones. The re-building of the German army, navy and air force, the occupation of the Ruhr, the Anschluss of Austria, the Munich Conference, followed by the occupation of Czechoslovakia.

By then, he, like many of his military colleagues, was convinced that Hitler was a shrewd and acceptable leader, though lacking in class and education. He felt that the Soviet-German Non-Aggression Pact was a diplomatic marvel and a great coup for Germany. He knew that the Red Army and the *Reichswehr* had had secret agreements of long standing—many of which had been started by the Weimar Republic long before Hitler. (This is factually correct. German army units had held secret maneuvers on Soviet territory for years, starting in the early 1920s in defiance of the Versailles Treaty).

Like many of his military comrades, he believed that a permanent accommodation between Germany and the Soviet Union was entirely possible. By the time Poland, France and most of Europe had been captured, the General's adjective for Hitler had changed from "acceptable" to "admirable".

Anti-Semitism was not a major concern for the General. There had been very few Jews in the professional army prior to Hitler and none since. He never gave them much thought. Yes, he knew of the Nuremberg Laws. He considered them a bit excessive at the time but as long as the Jews obeyed them, there were no great problems. Besides, he thought if the Jews wanted to leave Germany, they should just do so. He disliked the SA and the SS, they were uneducated rabble, but he knew it was unwise to voice these feelings.

All this changed with Hitler's decision to invade Russia. The General had served in the conquest of France and now was given command of a division on the Eastern Front. By the fall of 1941, deep into Soviet territory, he was appalled by the treatment of the civilian population. Not only was the army ordered to be ruthless regarding prisoners, but he now saw SS units under Himmler systematically rounding up civilians and shooting many on the spot. The first winter of the German invasion of the Soviet Union—

the winter of 1941—was a horror for the German army. They had expected to be in Moscow and Leningrad by the beginning of the cold weather. Consequently, no winter uniforms or special equipment had been issued to the troops. Now the army was stopped and had to endure the cruel Russian winter in the open fields. Without sufficient warm clothing, many men suffered frostbites and the casualties both from the inclement weather and the Red Army were enormous.

The General's final and, evidently, major disillusionment with the Nazi government came a few months later. I had asked him about atrocities committed by the German army, not just the SS. He was silent for a while, then he looked up and said: "In the spring of '43 after a short but very intense firefight, a Soviet battalion surrendered to my unit. Disarmed, the prisoners were marched to my headquarters.

I called to the rear for guards and supplies to deal with so many men. I was told there were no guards available and at the same time I was ordered to resume our attack. I called back and complained that I could not go on the attack with some 600 Soviet soldiers unguarded at my back. The response was to dispose of the prisoners and move on.

I called once more for specific instructions. This time the response was curt and threatening: "There are to be no prisoners left behind. You are to resume the attack immediately. Dispose of the prisoners as ordered, or face court martial."

I had a choice and chose the easy way. The prisoners were machine-gunned. I believe a few escaped."

"Did he know of the concentration camps?"

"Yes, of course. They were started as early as 1933. "Enemies of the Third Reich" were incarcerated for an indefinite period, often terribly mistreated. Yes, some were even killed but, by and large, most were eventually released. Later around 1944, he heard that the concentration camps had become extermination camps. Those were terrible stories and he hoped they were not true.

"Had he been to any camp? Had he been to Dachau?"

"No."

"Well," I told him, "I had been there just four weeks earlier. My unit arrived at Dachau a few hours after it had been liberated. The gates of the camp were wide open. The guards had already been arrested or killed. Thousands of people were roaming through the camp like skeletons. The inmates were all men—some of Asian descent— probably Soviet prisoners.

"All of them must have been starved for months to be so weak and skinny. Few spoke or understood English. All were disoriented, shuffling along silently and aimlessly in their striped uniforms. Some seemed to be aware that they were now free, but they had nowhere to go and did not know what to do. The pain from hunger and untreated illnesses screamed from every face. They came up to us hoping for food. A few had already gotten some from the unit that had freed the camp.

"Now we were told not give them any food because their weakened bodies would be unable to digest it and they would die in terrible agony. Only very special alimentation could save them. In fact, I saw a number of these unfortunate people moaning in painful convulsions on the ground. It was an indescribable feeling to be in the midst of so much suffering and not be able to help. We were assured that a medical team was on the way, but we did not stay long enough to see them.

"I saw the crematoria—they were not in use when I arrived. A railroad track ran from the ovens to the rear exit of the camp, and a train of six or seven open freight cars—the locomotive derailed—stood silently on the tracks. Evidently, it had been caught in an attempt to leave the camp.

"Even at this late stage of the war, the Germans were trying to hide evidence of their atrocities. The cars were open flat beds with five-foot poles mounted vertically to contain the cargo. Each car was loaded with naked corpses, thrown willy-nilly onto the cars. Layers and layers of arms, legs, torsos—once human beings—were dangling from the cars—grim evidence of Nazi insanity. It was an unforgettable—and in its magnitude—an indescribable horror." This is what I told the General. He listened, never said a word, and asked no questions. He was clearly shaken. And that is what was so troubling. Here I was, face to face with a war criminal, yet he seemed to have a conscience. He seemed kind, cultured, friendly and apologetic. Was he a monster? A victim? To this day I have no answers. I only wonder how I would have acted had I been in his shoes.

These talks went on for several evenings. They were very odd indeed. There was no shouting, no personal accusations from me, no absurd denials from him. Here was a man old enough to be my father, much higher in rank than me, telling me of his experiences and, in a way, confessing his sins. It had the unreal feeling as if we were in one of the old World War I movies, where the bitter enemies meet and treat each other with honor and respect.

All this ended when orders came that all Colonels and Generals were to be moved to a new location. Before leaving, my General came to me for permission to have a private word. "I remember," he said, "when I surrendered to you that afternoon, you looked at my scarf and I feared you would take it from me. It was very special to me—a gift from my wife—a talisman to protect me. Now the war is over and I won't need it any more and I would like to give it to you."

I took the scarf, we saluted and that was the last I saw of my General. I wore the scarf from that day on. Soon the U.S. Military Government took control of the area and the prison camp was turned over to them.

34

My next assignment was more exciting. The police chief of Munich—a notorious war criminal—had escaped arrest. There were rumors that he was hiding in the area. We were assigned to find him. Johnny Baer, Lt. Sternberg and I began to ask civilians about the whereabouts of this man. We had pictures of him and many locals knew him by name. We received constant tips. He had been seen in a local hotel, in a bar, in Nuremberg.

It was interesting how eager the population was to co-operate with us even when they had no useful information. At that time there were no Nazis in Germany. Everyone had a story to tell of how they were opposed to that terrible regime and how happy they were that it was now over. Ironic how this just-so-recent master race now subserviently accepted their conquerors.

Eventually, we received a more specific tip. There was a farm a few kilometers from Munich, which employed released prisoners of war for farm work. The wanted man was said to be among them. Johnny, Lt. Sternberg and I changed into local shabby civilian clothes and arrived at the farm about noon in time for the main meal.

Some 20 men came from the fields and sat at a long wooden table in the farmyard. We had already spoken with the farm owner, identifying ourselves as American officers and assuring him that we were there merely to see that everything was in good order and that we anticipated no problems.

So, as the men sat down to eat, we joined them. Most were in their 20s and 30s. Only a few were clearly older but none resembled the picture we had of Hueber—not his real name, which I have since forgotten.

When most of the talk gave way to eating, I suddenly shouted: "Polizei President Hueber, stand up!" We were watching the older men. One was so startled that he dropped his spoon. With pistols drawn, we arrested him. There was no resistance. We were quite lucky. Had he been armed, we might have started a firefight but as it was, we had our man and turned him over to the Military Government.

A few weeks later, I had to go to Nuremberg. The bombed out autobahn had been repaired sufficiently and I was driving my jeep at a good clip when I saw what appeared to be a hitchhiker. I slammed on my brakes and backed up a bit. Sure enough, a middle-aged German civilian was asking for a ride. Now that was totally unacceptable. There was a general "Reiseverbot" (travel restriction) in place throughout the American sector, and no German was allowed to be on the roads without a travel permit. Permits were not granted unless one could show by what means one intended to travel (bicycle, horse cart, etc).

Obviously, this man had no permit but had the guts (chutzpah!) to hitch hike and to ask for a ride from an American Army vehicle. I asked for his permit and, of course, he had none. Why was he on the road and where was he headed? He was on his way to Nuremberg, he said, to meet his son, who had just been released by the Americans because he was ill. As a father, he was anxious to help.

Why hadn't he asked for a travel permit? Clearly, he had a good reason and would be issued one. "Oh," he replied, "I'd never get one. For years I've been avoiding the Nazi authorities here in Munich. I've been active in the movement against the war. They know me. I would never get a travel permit."

"Well," I said, "that's nonsense. The Americans certainly don't know you; so let's find out what really is going on. I took him in my jeep and turned around, and headed back to Munich. We arrived at Military Government only to be told that Travel Permits were no longer issued by them.

That job had now been turned over to the police. They gave me the address and as I stormed into the police offices past several secretaries looking for the person issuing the permits, I was directed through a private door to a large officiously decorated room. There, behind an enormous desk sat the very police chief whom I had arrested less than a month ago. There he was—as powerful as ever. I was speechless. I turned around and drove back to the Military Government.

My loud complaints were answered with: "We know, we know, but we need someone to keep the city under control, and this man knows his way around. He is very cooperative and very useful." Disgusted, I left with my hitchhiker in tow. I ordered a travel permit for him and drove him to Nuremberg.

This was an enormous shock. Obviously, this had not been a local decision. This had come from the top. So just weeks after the end of this very, very bloody war, we were coddling known war criminals, just because they were "useful". This marked the first time I began to wonder whether I wanted to stay in Germany to aid in the "Denazification" process.

Many years later I learned that we used many of these "useful" ex-Nazis, and often rewarded them by offering them important positions in science, politics and commerce, i.e., Werner von Braun— a German rocket scientist who had been a Nazi. As the Cold War progressed, both sides were guilty of this shameful behavior.

The German government, under surveillance of the Allies, was not much better. Germany held a number of trials for Nazi politicians and judges. Most of them received life sentences or very lengthy prison terms. None eventually served more than five years! "Denazification" came to a sudden halt when the then German chancellor Adenauer famously announced: We must stop putting our nose into the smelly Nazi past or we will come out stinking ourselves.

35

It was early June, I believe, when Switzerland, which had strictly observed its neutrality, now allowed former combatants to visit their country. As soon as I heard this, I asked for a leave to go to Neuchatel. Almost immediately, I received orders to report to Army headquarters in Nuremberg. I was very excited about the prospect of seeing Jeanette and happy that my request had been acted upon so promptly.

At headquarters I was told that I was to report to General Patton. Proudly, I appeared before the General with a brisk salute. Seated behind a desk, Patton eyed me coldly then said: "Captain, you're out of uniform. Remove that red scarf immediately."

That scolding was followed by a brief interrogation: "Didn't you just have a leave for Paris?"

"Yes, Sir."

"Well, what is this new request? What kind of officer asks for constant leaves? Shirks his duties?"

"Well, Sir..." I tried to explain but got no further.

"Leave denied. Dismissed. Good day, Captain."

Patton won that round, but I won, too. Within five minutes I had the scarf back around my neck. I wore it all the way home to the U.S. Patton might have been a good general, but in my opinion, he was not a good person. He famously slapped a shell-shocked GI in a hospital calling him a coward, but even more sinister was Patton's address to all the officers of the Third Army shortly after the end of the war. He had ordered us all onto a huge field where, aided by numerous loudspeakers, we were subjected to an hour-long tirade. The gist was this: officers, do not ask to be demobilized. The war is not over. We have fought the wrong enemy. Our real enemy is to the East.

What a disgusting performance. We all knew that the war was won primarily by the Soviet Union's enormous sacrifices. Only a few weeks earlier General Eisenhower had praised the "Glorious Red Army". We all had seen photos of the U.S. and USSR soldiers jubilantly dancing together upon the meeting at the Elbe River. Now Patton proposed his own foreign policy of treachery. Fortunately, he met his end in a fatal car crash shortly after this episode.

Back in Munich, my original unit was now dissolved. Both Sternberg and Baer had asked for immediate demobilization and the rest of the men had been dispersed to various other duties. Soon I got new orders: "Take temporary control of the city of Augsburg."

It was an insane assignment. I had no staff, no office, no idea what I was expected to do. Augsburg had about 100,000 inhabitants. Like most cities, it had been bombed severely and the rubble was everywhere. Military Government contacted me and told me simply to be available. Soon they would send their own team to take over. So my job was to be there.

On the first day I drove through the outskirts and found a deserted military compound—"Eine Kaserne" as in "Lilli Marlene". It had a stable (the German army still kept a some horses), and the old stable master—a sergeant—had stayed on to take care of the animals.

Looking at the stables, I remembered my humiliating horse-backing riding experience in Griffith Park in Los Angeles. So I went over to the sergeant and told him that I wanted to learn how to ride properly. He was to give me instructions. With nothing else to do, I spent the next three weeks daily at the stable. The sergeant had picked a young filly as the suitable horse for me. Every morning we spent at least two hours at the ring. First, I had to learn to ride bareback—not an easy task for a beginner. Later, he put both the horse and me through the drills of different gaits. The old sergeant was a very friendly guy, totally apolitical, and we never spoke of anything but horses.

This was very unusual because there was a great shortage of everything, food and clothing, throughout the land, and as soon one was involved in a conversation with a German, one was told how anti-Nazi he or she had been and that was immediately followed by a request for some favor. Not my sergeant. He was always grateful for whatever I gave him but never subservient.

In the afternoons, we usually took cross-country rides for a few hours. Not much happened in those days and, thus, my memory is somewhat blurred. There must have been some unofficial German authority in town because I was never asked to preside over anything. Military Government took its time; they did not take over for several months.

36

As time passed, I began to realize that there was not much for me to do in Germany so I asked to be demobilized. Just before leaving Augsburg, I met a Hungarian girl. She was a refugee, anxious to get out of Europe and had asked for my help. She was very beautiful, very vulnerable, and very available.

Her story was both typical for the time and very sad. Her husband, the father of the three-year-old little girl she carried along, had been in the Hungarian army and been killed in Russia. She and her little girl had fled from the Russians and had walked and hitchhiked into Austria and eventually Germany. She hoped that the American authorities would listen to her plight and allow her to immigrate to the U.S.

For several weeks I tried to help her get a visa but with no success. Only the awareness of soon seeing Albertine had stopped me from starting a serious relationship. When I left, I gave her my Los Angeles address. A few months later I received a desperate letter from her, but there was nothing I could do to help her at that point.

Which brings me to the story of Albertine, so rarely mentioned in this account. Every army tries to boost the morale of its soldiers and nothing does the job better than mail delivery from home. For the U.S. army, this was of prime importance and "mail call" was almost a daily event, even for us in combat. After leaving

Philadelphia, Alix—or "Dopple" as I called her—and I, had written each other two or three times a week. What I wrote and what she responded is long lost and forgotten. One can be certain that they were mostly love letters full of dreams for the future.

During the first few weeks of the invasion, writing letters was not possible, and later just trying to survive was more important. Although, of course, I wrote when we were not in active battle, I could not mention anything dealing with the war. Receiving letters from home was another story. And, of course, a very welcome one. Both Alix and my mother wrote often—frequently asking for more letters from me.

It never really occurred to me that not to communicate was inconsiderate, that at home they were worried and hoping daily for news. After the end of the war, I had received letters from my mother and a few from Alix. They knew I was toying with the thought of staying in Europe. Alix said it would be my decision but she never really indicated how she felt about the idea. Now I wrote them I was ready to return to the U.S.

I had asked to be de-mobilized in Philadelphia and by late October I got passage on one of the Queen ships from Hamburg to New York and from there to Camp Kilmer, N.J., for final dismissal. From New York, I had called Albertine, but no one was in. So the next call was to Goetz and Lucy. Lucy answered the phone. After brief happy greetings, she asked what my plans were. Well, I would be out in a few days and would be in Philadelphia before the end of the week. I told her that I had called Albertine but that she was not in.

Lucy was quiet for a moment and then said: "You know, Walter, it might be best if you didn't come to Philadelphia. Albertine has met someone here and she doesn't want to see you right now. Of course, you can come to visit with us. That's up to you."

Naturally, I wanted some details. So I learned that Albertine had been in therapy partly over concerns for me at the front and over time, she had fallen in love with her therapist. End of story. Lucy was very kind, but what could she say. So I thanked her and hung up. I was very confused and stunned. Of course, the relationship with Albertine had been very brief but I was looking forward to being with her. In Germany there had been a number of dalliances, all very meaningless. Now the great "after-the-war-life" looked very cold and empty.

At Camp Kilmer I asked to be demobilized in Los Angeles. Kilmer was a huge place filled with thousands of soldiers—all waiting to leave the army. We were housed in barracks, hundreds of men in each one—all of different units and ranks. All of us were just waiting for transportation.

Every morning, a list was posted with the names for whom transportation to their desired destination had been provided. I was in the shower when I heard a new list had just been posted. Naked I ran to see if my name was on the list. Yes, I was to be on a plane for L.A. by 11 a.m. As I went back to get dressed, my red and gold scarf was missing. It was one of the few souvenirs I had hoped to keep. Now it was gone in the mad disorder of Camp Kilmer. It was hopeless to try to find the thief.

Back in Los Angeles, I was properly discharged. Routinely, they asked me if I wanted to stay in the Army Reserve. It would mean a few weeks training each year but basically that would be it. I would keep my rank and eventually be available for promotion. Some day, when I reached 62, I would be eligible for a small pension. The decision was easy. We had defeated the Nazis and the Japanese. There were no enemies left, there would be no more wars. Gladly, I accepted and found myself out of active service and in the Reserve.

Late in 2011, just about as I was finishing writing these recollections, I found a letter from a Thomas Maeder. It was dated 1982, tucked away in a folder of "letters to be answered." Evidently, I had forgotten about it.

Mr. Maeder had written me because he was doing research for a book, dealing with the fate of children of psychologists. Since both of his parents were psychologists, he began by looking at documents his deceased mother had stashed away. There he had found a bundle of about 100 letters from a Lt. Bodlander to Albertine, his mother. Somewhat apologetically, he wrote that he had read all of them—they were love letters sent during the war. Would I be interested to re-read them?

My love for Albertine was—by 1982—a lifetime behind me. I had since been married twice and the emotions of a long ago love were deeply buried. I had found Mr. Maeder's letter very interesting and I must have intended to answer him eventually but never got around to it. Now, re-discovering his missive and much involved in the memories of the war years, I certainly wanted to see and read my old notes to Albertine. But this was 2011—29 years later! Where was Mr. Maeder and how could I find him? Google came to the rescue.

Mr. Maeder had, indeed, written the intended book and many others as well and he had several publishers. I contacted them, told them my reason to try to locate the author and one of them agreed to relay my address and phone number to him. Two days later I spoke with him and he very kindly agreed to send me the letters.

It was embarrassing to read those rather juvenile notes. They contained very little about the war or the conditions and feelings of the moment. Certainly, I must have been aware of the strict restraints imposed by wartime censorship and that would be the only excuse for these rather boring uninspired V-mails. Mostly they were love letters, dreaming of a future, which was never to be.

Thus ends the first part of my memoirs. My subsequent life may be much less interesting to potential readers, so those recollections can wait for awhile. If I write about the later years, I will not go into too much detail but just mention a few experiences—the highs and the lows.